Live an Adventure

David M King

David M King

MEREO
Cirencester

Mereo Books
1A The Wool Market Dyer Street Cirencester Gloucestershire GL7 2PR
An imprint of Memoirs Publishing www.mereobooks.com

LIVE AN ADVENTURE: 978-1-86151-867-5

First published in Great Britain in 2018
by Mereo Books, an imprint of Memoirs Publishing

Copyright ©2018

David M King has asserted his right under the Copyright Designs and Patents Act 1988 to be identified as the author of this work.

A CIP catalogue record for this book is available from the British Library.

This book is sold subject to the condition that it shall not by way of trade or otherwise be lent, resold, hired out or otherwise circulated without the publisher's prior consent in any form of binding or cover, other than that in which it is published and without a similar condition, including this condition being imposed on the subsequent purchaser.

The address for Memoirs Publishing Group Limited can be found at
www.memoirspublishing.com

The Memoirs Publishing Group Ltd Reg. No. 7834348

The Memoirs Publishing Group supports both The Forest Stewardship Council® (FSC®) and the PEFC® leading international forest-certification organisations. Our books carrying both the FSC label and the PEFC® and are printed on FSC®-certified paper. FSC® is the only forest-certification scheme supported by the leading environmental organisations including Greenpeace. Our paper procurement policy can be found at www.memoirspublishing.com/environment

Typeset in 12/18pt Century Schoolbook
by Wiltshire Associates Publisher Services Ltd. Printed and bound in Great Britain by Printondemand-Worldwide, Peterborough PE2 6XD

CONTENTS

	Introduction	
Chapter 1	Live an Adventure	1
Chapter 2	An Accidental Adventure	16
Chapter 3	To Thine Own Self Be True	41
Chapter 4	Be Holy, live Powerful	57
Chapter 5	Accountability and Team	71
Chapter 6	Never Give Up	86
Chapter 7	Dreams and Vision	101
Chapter 8	The Weapon of Forgiveness	119
Chapter 9	Amazing Grace	136
Chapter 10	Growth Mindset	146
Chapter 11	Trust and Betrayal	159
Chapter 12	Good Foundations	173
Chapter 13	Strengths and Weaknesses	185
Chapter 14	The importance of Character	198
Chapter 15	Legacy	211
Chapter 16	To Eternity and Beyond!	220

Introduction

Life can be mundane, ordinary or awful – or it can be an adventure. I am sharing my story to hopefully inspire you to live a life of adventure. Any adventure will almost certainly involve moments you would rather not experience. However, going through them can strengthen you and help you to grow. It can also reveal how significant your adventure is.

The dictionary defines adventures as unusual, exciting or daring experiences. Excitement associated with danger or the taking of risks: *she travelled the world in search of adventure.* An adventure is a reckless or potentially hazardous action or enterprise.

Any adventure involves overcoming failure. If you want to successfully move through a failure, you must maintain your attitude while controlling your emotions. Failure can stir many different emotions, like anger or frustration. Having these emotions is normal. However, to succeed in your adventure you can't allow your emotions to cause you to react negatively or have a bad attitude. Controlling our emotions and attitudes requires self-awareness and self-control. During a failure, focus. Put your effort into cultivating a positive, optimistic attitude. Acknowledge your emotions, but don't allow them to drive your life or your adventure, your actions or attitude. Focus on the adventure, not the difficulties.

My story is my adventure. Because it is my story, you will find many references to the Gospel and the church. Don't be put off. Each adventure is valid and personal. It is just my experience. For me at least, the most exciting adventure of all is one that does not merely focus on this life but also on eternity and beyond (to nearly quote from a famous film). Whatever your adventure, I trust you will find helps, hints and concepts which progress you forward. I encourage you to see each chapter as another tool to add to your tool box to empower you to live an adventure for yourself. Most of all though, I trust that my adventure will encourage you to explore Christ, His claims and His church, with a view to including these in your adventure. Remember, the best is yet to come!

Love and blessings

David
www.davidandlindaking.org
davidmking.author@gmail.com

CHAPTER 1
Live an adventure

Wherever you are in life, no matter how old or how young, your life is an adventure. It's never too late to live it as one. I share my story with you in the hope that it inspires you to live your adventure, no matter how inauspicious your beginning. I believe that you, like me, can still transform your future and live an adventure. As C.S. Lewis wrote: "*You can't go back and change the beginning but you can start where you are and change the ending*".

To live well we need to know at the very heart of our 'knower'! We are not just people who are born on the planet or even born again (John 3:3-6). We are people of identity, purpose and destiny. God has predestined us to fulfil his plans on the earth. *"It has always been God's unchanging plan to God-adopt us into his own family by bringing us to himself through Jesus Christ. This is what he wanted to do and this gave him great pleasure."* (Ephesians 1:5)

The world we live in hasn't got time for us to be on the 'back foot' drifting through life. We and the world need to know that we know who we are. Then we can influence the world around us for good. We are to bring life to ourselves and to everyone within our sphere of influence. We are to be proactive, not passive, not over worried about making mistakes. As a follower of Christ, or even as a human being on this planet, WE experience some 'wow' moments, or as Linda and I call them, "pinch me" moments. Moments that take us out of the ordinary and into the extraordinary.

So who are you? Who am I? We, if we dare to believe it, are adventurers, explorers, discovers and 'creatives'. My adventure began in less than inspiring circumstances. I was born just after the Second World War. It was a time of rationing, a time before the National Health Service, and I was born with a cleft palate. This led me into an adventure which was, as is often the case, an adventure I did not choose or even want. My adventure involved fighting to be understood first by my family, then friends, then by the world around me. This adventure and the fight continue, but now I know I am "a new creation." I am born again to push back obstacles and barriers, born to be all I can possibly be in the power of God's Spirit. This is what it truly means to be born again or born from above (John 3:3-6). No longer do natural limitations define my life. I have a second birth; a new birthright!

This world seeks to define our identity in independence selfishness and rebellion. This leads to isolation and separation. In the words of a famous song *"I'll do it my way!"* However, God's way is one of connection of unity and oneness. My adventure of being an adventurer, discoverer, explorer and overcomer is to work to see others flourish and be fulfilled, living out of their identity. Mother Teresa wrote *"I alone cannot change the world, but I can cast a stone across the water to create many ripples."* Not that we have to be Mother Teresas, but we do have our own adventure to live as special and extra-ordinary people.

To live an adventure is to embrace the extraordinary. Adventurers refuse to settle in boredom for a mundane life. If I know who I am, I can live a life of honour, honouring myself and everyone around me. Honour involves giving value and worth.

Honour involves living responsibly, understanding the consequences of our actions and clearing up our own messes.

If life is not an adventure, then perhaps it is compartmentalised. Then instead of an adventure, life is sub-divided into work, family, social, sport, church etc. Maybe that is how some live, even as Christians.

What is an adventure? It is going towards a goal or destination, whatever happens along the way. Sometimes, like Abraham and the men of faith (Hebrews 11, esp. v13) we do not really know where we are going. However we are looking for a city (Hebrews 11:8-10; 13-16). Imagine going to a city you cannot physically see. Perhaps like a wagon train going across the west or explorers going across the sea; some give up. Our journey, our adventure, is achieving something beyond this world. However, it seems too hard; some lose their sense of adventure, abandon the journey and settle – it's all just too hard!

Living the adventure that is Christ is journeying into something of ultimate value and purpose. We may meet deceivers or enemies in various forms. We may have to cross difficult terrain; care for families and individuals. Our adventure involves encouraging, supporting, and fighting for ourselves and others. What an adventure we are called to! Is it merely seeing people saved? As a famous preacher once said *"OK, you are saved, now I will shoot you so you can just go to heaven!"* Is that all the gospel is? Just be saved and stop? Or is it following the adventure that is Christ?

Jesus said "follow me". He took his disciples on an amazing, twisting, turning adventure. A journey of miracles, despair, joy, defeat and ultimate victory. Come live the adventure that is Christ. This may involve having to face down powerful demons, who seek to persuade me to accept a negative, destructive, ungodly destiny for my life. To resist strong, spiritual powers, overcome deceit. Sometimes personally I lose ground and people to them, but the adventure calls me onward. Death, destruction, pain, suffering, broken relationships, destroyed lives; false values and false belief systems constantly bombard me, but that is part of the adventure. If the gospel and following Christ are not an adventure, then what are they? It becomes my truth v. a negative "truth". However God's truth is bigger, better, than negative "truth".

An adventure involves going deeper than living superficial lives. To enjoy our adventure, it is important to understand shame and its effects. Whether we believe in God and His word or not, we are all affected by shame from our birth. Shame tells us we are wrong. Shame says I'm the problem at some stage of our life, depending on circumstances, events and relationships. Shame is the intensely painful feeling or experience of believing we are flawed, therefore unworthy of being loved or belonging. It is the fear of disconnection. Learning to be shame-resilient empowers us to connect with people in a life-affirming and relevant way. Understanding shame and becoming equipped in shame resilience enables the Gospel to be not just spiritual but an emotional, mental and spiritual transformation, which it is what it is intended to be.

Because of the fall we are born with shame (Genesis 3). When we are small someone else initiates shame in us. In some kind of way they send us a message that we are not enough, not good enough, not sufficient. Note – it doesn't need to be true in itself or even intended – the issue is the way we perceive it, and agree with it.

When we live in agreement consciously, or unconsciously with shame, we are destined to live with a shame identity of not feeling good enough and not being able to see a way out. Everything we do seems to confirm our shame identity. Life itself becomes more and more hard, or even meaningless. To cope we cover our shame with material possessions or addictive lifestyles. We seek success or popularity, but these have no roots in themselves, and our lives continue to feel empty. When we live in the circumstances of life, we seek to survive by fight or flight. Shame is felt in the emotions as pain – it hurts! So because I feel pain in my emotions, the adrenalin kicks in and I will want to either fight or take flight – push others away (or even push myself away from myself – self-hatred). The roots of shame is what we believe in our minds. This is where the battle is (Romans 12:2). It's like tapes playing in your mind telling you what a failure you are, no good, weak, useless etc. This self-talk needs to be transformed.

Shame resilience involves being proactive and understanding the connection between our emotions and our thinking.

Two men looked through prison bars; one saw mud, the other saw stars. As we get older we develop these shame messages all on our own. Whether it's real or imagined, it has the same impact on us. As we go along, things people say or situations subconsciously can send us right back to those early incidents of shame, and our behaviour kicks in accordingly. Sometimes other people may be left wondering – what happened there? (disconnection). Everyone is born like a caterpillar, with an instinct to exist and survive, but we can't fly yet. Hence Jesus said we must be born from above or born again (John 3:3-6). This involves being born spiritually of water and the Spirit – The spirit to bring us into freedom, purpose and destiny and water to give us a new identity in Christ. We become butterflies, able to be seated in Heavenly places (Ephesians 2:5-6).

Hope empowers shame resilience. Hope affirms my identity. Hope says 'I have worth, I am valuable, special and precious and my life has meaning and purpose'. Our life is to be lived from adventure, not merely incidents. Whether people understand me or love me does not determine my worth or value. My worth is determined by God. He said my life (like your life) was worth the death of His Son on the cross. Not only that, He proved it by raising Jesus from the dead so that I too can live eternally with Him by grace through faith.

Shame resilience involves learning to normalise shame.

a) Recognise that shame is universal – we all have it. I can only recognise shame at work if I accept the truth that it affects me (see the fall). It is universal – I have it!

b) Recognise our vulnerable areas (or triggers). Get to know what your triggers are.

c) Recognise your shame behaviour – what does your behaviour look like when you feel shame? What do you do? I would want to withdraw. Other classic behaviours are aggression, blaming, shaming, appeasing, trying to please, doing things to make others like you; avoiding confrontation at all costs. So never challenge or question others.

d) Talk about it to someone "safe". It will be helpful if you can ask someone to lovingly tell you or ask questions like 'What are you feeling?' What are you thinking right now? Why are you behaving like this? Just normalise your feelings of shame and it will start to free you up. There is no shame in shame. There is no shame in feeling shame. So normalise your feelings of shame – 'I feel shame at this moment' will help you to move into freedom and feel better about yourself.

Remember other people – feel, think ,experience and behave out of shame – they have similar feelings to you – You are normal! I am normal! Feelings and experience of shame are normal!

> Shame resilience separates guilt from shame.
> Put very simply:
> GUILT – I DID something wrong.
> SHAME – I AM wrong.

Why does this matter? If I DID something wrong I can ask forgiveness and correct it. If I AM wrong – if there is something intrinsically wrong with me, there is nothing I can do about it. If I mix up guilt and shame, after a while I will become more and more powerless to change my behaviour. When I DO something wrong I increasingly believe I AM wrong. I condemn myself and find it increasingly difficult to change my behaviour.

Conversely, if I separate guilt from shame I can ask forgiveness, be held accountable and learn, grow and seek to correct my mistakes. I can work on powerful ways to be resilient to the lies that seek to shame me. This is why the understanding of whom we are in Christ and that we are 'unpunishable' is so significant. Christ has borne ALL the punishment for ALL my sin for ALL time (Isaiah 53 etc). This truth frees me to avoid hiding and instead to face any mistakes I make and grow and learn how to correct them.

When we live out of adventure we learn to separate guilt and shame and deal with them differently. Adventure means owning your story. If you own it, you get to interact in it. You get to be powerful in it. You get to agree with and live from God's planned destiny for your life. You write the ending! When you are proactive in your adventure, you take authority to write your story without shame (author – authority – author-ority)! You change things you need to change and value who you are. Carl Jung said "*I am not what has happened to me, I am what I choose to become.*" Father, God, Jesus and the Holy Spirit say – "*You are not what has happened to you – You are my beloved son with a future and a hope.*"

Who do you think you are? How you respond can lead to adventure or existence. I am an imperfect, loved child of God – with all that goes with that.

It was God's unchanging plan to adopt me into His family, and that gave Him great pleasure (Ephesians 1:5).

I cannot be a failure!

I do not have to be perfect – perfectionism is not a requirement. God loves and accepts me as I am (warts and all).

Shame resilience means we must love ourselves as God does. Keep practising to be kind to ourselves and accept His covering of us.

Hand in hand with love we must understand honour.

I am a saint, a holy one (Ephesians 1:1).

I have been adopted as God's child (Ephesians 1:5).

I have direct access to God through the Holy Spirit (Ephesians 2:18).

I have been redeemed and forgiven for all my sins (Colossians 1:14).

I am complete in Christ (Colossians 2:10).

Live an adventure. Don't merely absorb the world's view or attitudes to life and life's experiences. Choose life. Be a person of life and love – affect the world, rather than merely being affected or influenced by it! Take responsibility and own consequences of your actions. Know your identity and purpose, and destiny in Christ is assured.

HERO	ZERO
Honour – Unpunishable; justified; grace; growth mindset; being transformed into the likeness of Christ; creative, prophetic, think outside the box	**Zilch** – Shame; worthless; Punish; Law; force; position; coarse humour; belittle, mock, put down victim mentality; follow 'orders', don't ask questions; fixed mindset – I am what I am. Resist change – I can't change!
Experience – What happens; hope, faith, kingdom identity; seek reasons, ask questions, be an agent of change	**Experience** – what happens; identity from natural world; boredom, powerlessness, passive acceptance, follow rules, don't think for yourself
Reaction (Godly) Passion and love for God; seeking first His Kingdom & His righteousness; support; encouragement, confidence, seek reasons, empower to overcome, I am who God says, I am not who the world says I am – I am more than a conqueror, I am a son loved and precious	**Reaction** (Earthly) Obey orders; don't challenge; do what is asked; bystander effect – watch, wait, do nothing! Don't challenge passivity, pass the blame, not my fault, nothing to do with me! Retaliate. It's all my fault I'm worthless & useless, I never do anything right.
Outcome – Fruit; blessings; self-worth; self respect; true to God and self; love, forgiveness grace acceptance	**Outcome** – disappointment; sense of failure; guilt, pain, punishment, fear

To actively live an adventure is to be fruitful. As in nature, there are many different kinds of fruit. You will never get the fruit of a banana from an apple tree, nor will you get a large potato crop in the wrong soil. So to live well, we need to understand our God-given identity and live well from that identity. It is not enough to be busy; we are destined for effectiveness and fruitfulness. To be fruitful we need to ensure we are planted in the right soil in the right conditions; or in the words of Jim Collins – "we need to know we are the right people sitting in the right seat on the right bus going in the right direction." (*Good to Great*, by Jim Collins). For instance I know I am not a 'DIYer'; it is best for me not to offer help on a DIY project – it will save everyone time and energy! However I know I am prophetic and a world changer. Living well involves not trying to keep everyone happy; it is about ensuring you keep Him happy! IE you do what God has called you to do rather than do it because it needs doing. Don't be afraid not to be - be what and who you are. Leaders are people who influence others. You influence whether you smile, groan or complain. You are an influence on other people and your environment. Even if you live on a desert island, you influence your environment.

I urge you to recognise and accept that you are living an adventure, a life of discovery and exploration.

You are a 'creative' made by a creator God. God believes in you; He has made you in His image to reflect His image to the world around you. You are God's love gift to the world. Don't hide in fear or insecurity. Don't hide - ride on his love. You are on an adventure; enjoy it – this book is written to encourage you.

Run the race set before you; there is no other person like you on the planet. You are one of the most important and influential people alive today on Planet Earth. You may or may not relate to some of my experiences, that's fine – we are all unique and no two people have exactly the same journey through life. This book is about pointing you to principles that you can apply whatever your calling and identity. You and I are called by God to change this fallen world for good. We are to be an influence for good. Learn to understand yourself – your inner dreams and desires, your passions, what gives you pleasure and excites you even from childhood. What are God's promises and prophetic words over your life? Go for them – live your adventure! God is able to do exceeding abundantly FAR BEYOND; all we could ask or imagine! God is not a limiting factor on you fulfilling your destiny or living well. God is GOOD! God is for you.

Some thoughts for your consideration

Are you willing to live an adventure?

What is stopping you from stepping into your adventure?

Can you be a hero in your adventure?
Why? Why not?

What has spoken to you most from this chapter?

CHAPTER 2
An accidental adventure

Most adventures are not planned – life just happens - so it is important to be on the front foot, to be proactive and not passive. It is not enough to say "whatever will be will be". The key element to changing from merely existing to living an adventure is our mindset.

A scholar asked a boatman to row him across the river. The journey was long and slow. The scholar was bored. "Boatman," he called out "Let's have a conversation." Suggesting a topic of special interest to himself, he asked "Have you ever studied phonetics or grammar?"

"No" said the boatman. "I've no use for those tools."

"Too bad," said the scholar. "You've wasted half your life. It's useful to know the rules."

Later the rickety boat crashed into a rock in the middle of the river. The boatman turned to the scholar and said "Pardon my humble mind that to you must seem dim, but wise man, tell me have you ever learned to swim?"

"No" said the scholar, "I've never learned. I've immersed myself in thinking."

"In that case," said the boatman, "you've wasted all your life. Alas, the boat is sinking."

Living an adventure involves us in learning and stretching ourselves; this may mean (it did for me) overcoming rejection. We reinforce what we believe by the way we behave. Sometimes we think we believe something and even say we believe, but our behaviour reveals that in reality we believe something quite different. Going deeper helps us to recognise and acknowledge that all feelings are valid. However, feelings are transient. They are not reliable or consistent. Hence we don't have to act on them. They are merely our feelings at that time. As people of God we have feelings, but we are to be led by the Spirit of God not our feelings. Our values, lifestyle, behaviour and culture are formed out of the word of God, not our feelings.

Rejection can be real or imagined, and whichever it is inside of us, it has the same impact. After I was born, I spent months away from my family in Poole, having treatment at Great Ormond Street, London. Looking back, I know it was my family's love that sent me to London. However at the time, in my little heart I experienced rejection. This dogged me for years. Later in life I experienced real rejection. I was teased and bullied at school because I could not speak 'properly'. Many times I would cry myself to sleep. Even in adult life I found, and still do find, people saying hello and then quickly moving away or standing there moving their lips so they could understand me – it felt and feels humiliating and belittling and it empowered my rejection. I've learnt that rejection is rooted in one's self. Like all us I wanted to be liked and accepted. So inside, usually subconsciously, I would ask:

Am I OK?

Am I good enough?

Am I acceptable to others?

What do they really think of me?

What will they think if they find out what I am really like?

What will they think if I fail to......?

Rejection causes us to dislike or even hate ourselves. Our lives become a matter of existing from one event to another, outside our control. When this happens we become angry. We feel we fail God and others and try to cover up. It's hard to like yourself when you feel a failure. Rejection brings many temptations. For me, it was anger at myself for feeling weak and being unable even to speak clearly.

Once you have experienced rejection, you can identify it very quickly. I could pick it up as soon as I walked into a room. To minimise the pain of rejection we learn to reject others before they reject us. We say on the inside of us, albeit we don't really mean it, I don't care what you or they think. Rejection can lead to blaming, fault-finding and pointing the finger. Rejection gains its power when we live from existence instead of adventure. God delivered me through His love; He accepts me. He calls me amazing. I am called to live an amazing, adventurous life, a life in which I know the reality of being completely fulfilled in Christ.

Unbeknown to me, one of the inner lies God was already working on in me connected to rejection which I had absorbed. I am stupid! These lies gain power and strength when we see life as merely existence instead of an adventure. I had failed my eleven-plus exams. I left secondary modern school with no 'O' levels. This led me into a boring job. Eventually, seeking adventure, or at least something more than a boring job, I left. I returned to study and gained five 'O' levels at Poole College.

Some time after this I went to another college in Southampton to complete my accountancy studies. Before the finals, our lecturer spoke to my class. He spoke about who would probably pass and who would not and he never even mentioned me. Nervously, I asked "what about me?" "Oh, you will pass no problem!" he responded. Wow! No one apart from my mum had ever believed in me like that. Of course, I did pass my finals. I actually passed my full accountancy exams and became a qualified management accountant.

Much later, someone asked me to consider doing an MA. I thought they must be teasing. However the course interested me, so I enrolled. My accountancy qualification enabled me to be accepted on the course. In a sense God was working on my "strength" – that if I started something I was too stubborn to give up on it. I successfully completed six 5000-word essays on various subjects to gain a diploma. Then I was asked if I wanted to continue for my MA. I would need to produce a dissertation of 20,000 words for examination. Hesitantly I went for it. I experienced some setbacks, but eventually, in January 2012, I heard that I had been successful. Someone recently told me an MA is one of the highest academic qualifications. Not bad for someone stupid! So when you live your adventure, don't be defined by your past. Don't let lies stop you. Keep living your adventure. Failure is merely a path on the way to success.

Simon Sinek says: "*Whys are a belief. Hows are the actions you take to realise that belief and Whats are the results of those actions.*" What 'why' are you believing? What actions will you take – how? Living an adventure involves asking 'why not' things. Don't put yourself down or belittle yourself. Praise God for the person He has made you. We are all different but loved by God. When we say I am no good or I am not amazing, we disagree with God and belittle His creative gift. This can stop His power and heaven's resources from flowing through us to others. When we praise God and give Him glory for making us so amazing, we open the door to heaven's resources. We allow them to flow through us for the blessing of others and the nation. This is about who we are, NOT what we do. Being amazing makes us world changers. We are called amazing! Live an adventure.

Being amazing doesn't make life easy. For me, pain and sickness have come and disappointments occur, but I will not give up, and I encourage you not to. I have a Father who delights in me. He thinks I am special no matter what. That's why my relationship with Him is so important to me. I found an amazing woman who chose to love me. Even then, rejection dogged me. Our first year of marriage was a disaster. We only survived by the grace of God and our stubbornness that we would not divorce. If we had people round for a meal I would say nothing, for fear of not being understood. Linda had to do all the talking!

Towards the end of that first year I honestly felt God say to me, "tell your wife that you will not divorce her. Also tell her that God is number one in your life, not her". I did this. Immediately Linda said to me that that was exactly what she had sensed God was wanting her to tell me. This process brought real release and freedom to us both. We have now been married over 43 years, and although it is not perfect, it is getting better and better.

If you merely exist, life just happens. If you choose to live an adventure, you have to proactively accept your role and responsibilities. What do you think is one of your key roles? For me it is to fight in the Spirit for my wife, children and grandchildren. This is my call to arms, my adventure. It is spiritual warfare. Fight for her. Fight for your marriage. Fight for both your destinies. Call out her "birth gift" – your gifting (natural, not just learnt skills), calling and destiny. If you are single, you can do the following to your friends. If you are married, encourage your spouse in their gift – prophecy. Call it out of them (they may not see it yet). You are in this together. Your wife is your *Ezer Kenegdo*, your fellow warrior alongside you. Resist death and despair over her gifts and destiny. Their gift and destiny may really annoy you at times! In my case Linda has a teaching gift. She is interested in the detail. My gift is more visionary, prophetic and leadership-related. I just want to act, not keep explaining everything in great detail (at least that's how it can appear to me). Nevertheless, by sharing we get the best of both of us. I need the detail to earth me; she needs vision to rise up and believe for more. Don't focus on the annoyance; focus on the strengths. Remember God joined you together because He knew you could do more together than you could apart. This applies to singles and teams as well.

Listening is an active practice, not a passive one. When you listen, identify their feelings. Consider what they are really saying and listen for the story behind the story. For instance, when your wife tells you about a relationship conflict, what's usually your first impulse – fight or flight? How do you feel about a suggestion that you should affirm her feelings even if you disagree with her assessment of the situation and believe she's over-reacting? What might help you walk through the feelings with her? Out of some three billion men on Planet Earth, YOU are uniquely placed and empowered to fill your wife's emotional bank account. How does that make you feel?

What signals might tell you her emotional bank balance is empty or in overdraft?

What difference does it make when YOU affirm her and tell her she's beautiful?

Ladies, you can live an adventure. Do you know men (your man) needs to feel respected? How can you do this? How can you make him your hero?

Do you know men (your man) feels like an imposter? He is insecure about his inadequacies – how can you make him secure?

Men enjoy romance and want to be more romantic. However they hesitate, because they doubt they can succeed. Your sexual desire for your husband profoundly affects his sense of well-being and confidence in all areas of life.

In years gone by I've had to learn to recognise the enemy's destiny for my life. You may have to do the same. The root meaning of the word demon is 'distributor of destinies'. The enemy is a liar from the beginning. He is also a usurper. He seeks to usurp our God-given destiny. I had to come to a place of repentance. *"Lord I wake up to and repent of believing the enemies destinies for my life.* For me those destinies that went like *"only the lonely know how I feel"*. This was a Roy Orbison song that I would play over and over again on my record player in my bedroom. Another destiny was *"I think I will eat worms, long thin skinny ones, big fat juicy ones, think I'll live on worms"*. Rejection, isolation, unworthiness, were the enemies' destinies for my life.

Being born with a cleft palate enforced the power of these destinies on my life. *"No one will understand you"* – *"what's the point?"* – *"you are clumsy, you are stupid"* (having missed many years of school, this was easy to swallow!) The enemy destined me for heartache and loneliness. No one will ever love you! – The enemy seeks to divert each of us from God's identity and destiny. For me he wanted me to agree with and accept rejection, despair and hopelessness.

You and I have to learn to live an adventure – to accept and agree wholeheartedly with God's destiny for our life, no one else's. Receive His word and His promises. I am a son of the Father; nothing can ever separate me from the love of God in Christ. There is nothing I can do to make God love me more; there is nothing I can do to make God love me less! Nor can you. Living an adventure involves agreement. What or who are you agreeing with? You and I have a God-given identity. You and I are one of the most important and influential people alive today on Planet Earth (do you know you are too?) I have a prophetic calling to bring God's people into completeness in Christ. At my baptism I heard the words *"Open your mouth wide and I will fill it"* (Psalm 81:10). My response? No Lord, anything but that! Not with my speech impediment! Power is *"The ability to achieve our purpose and to effect change"* (Martin Luther King Jr). *No matter your past, you have the ability to create your tomorrow.* We live in a time of political turbulence and social division, which are challenging our common life. We desperately need a culture of encounter. Your calling is your calling; be true to it, live in the excitement and passion of it.

Why do we as humans crave for deep and meaningful relationships? It reflects the fact that we have been made by a God who enjoys a perfect relationship within Himself. A God who enjoys great love and wants to share that relationship with us. Personhood before productivity. Personhood is acknowledging that 'I'm a human being, not a human doing'. It is freedom to be; to embrace intentional uselessness and *"waste time with God."* Thomas Merton describes this well; *"The monk is not defined by his task his usefulness; in a certain sense he is supposed to be useless, because his mission is not to do this or that job but to be a man of God."*

Live the fullness of your adventure by developing emotional intelligence. Our soul consists of mind, will and emotions.

EMOTIONS

a) Emotions enable us to know and understand ourselves. We can't know God unless we know ourselves. The first commandment is to love God. Augustine wrote in Confessions in AD400: *"How can you draw close to God when you are far from your own self?"* Meister Eckhart, a Dominican writer from the thirteenth century, wrote: *"No one can know God who does not first know himself."* John Calvin wrote in 1530 in his opening of his "Institutes": *"Our wisdom... consists almost entirely of two parts the knowledge of God and of ourselves. But as these are connected together by many ties it is not easy to determine which of the two precedes and gives birth to the other."*

We can't know God unless we know ourselves; we can't love God unless we know Him.

There are four levels of loving God
(from William of Thierry):
1) Attraction/desire;
2) Clinging;
3) Enjoyment even in sorrow; and

4) Union of wills, where my will is one with His. *"He who the mind cannot grasp, the heart can embrace."*

Though we cannot understand God fully, we can hug Him. God leads every believer to the experience of Jesus in Psalm 22 and the cross. For this reason every wound is a grace. Wounds lead us to the fundamental level of self-knowledge. This leads to humility. This can then become love – the very centre of genuine spirituality.

b) Emotions enable us to know and love ourselves so we can love our neighbour as ourselves. The second commandment involves practising the presence of people. We cannot love our neighbour unless we love ourselves. We can't love ourselves unless we know ourselves. You may find it helpful to learn to keep an emotions journal: I feel ...... (now) When ...... (now experience) Why...... (past trigger) So...... (now action). An emotions journal enables us to keep in touch with how, why and what we feel. This enables us to identify areas of damage, which is a key step to being healed and whole.

c) Emotions help us identify our own hurt and have compassion to others. What an amazing privilege to walk with a Father God who loves us unconditionally! There is nothing I can do to make

God love me more. There is nothing I can do to make God love me less - whatever I feel, whatever I've done, whatever I've experienced, I am loved, chosen and adopted. Now I can learn not to hide in shame but be known and know Him fully, even as "damaged people being made whole." What an amazing Gospel for our broken and hurting world!

d) Emotions empower us to connect with others. Story helps our connections. Story encourages an action or decision and finds a place for our emotions. Story engages me to dreams, hopes, expectations and the faith that I or my circumstances can change. Story connects with the emotions and empowers them to move towards growth as we reveal the moral of the story.

e) Emotions help us handle loss. Loss is a foreign entity; we were not created to experience it. But as a result of the Fall, loss has become commonplace in all our lives, from the very significant to the mundane. Loss impacts us continually.

Loss is often experienced in the following progression:

1. DENIAL
2. ANGER/BLAMING
3. BARGAINING
4. DEPRESSION
5. ACCEPTANCE

No one else can make you feel what you feel!

The only way to genuinely understand your emotions is to spend time thinking them through to figure out what they are. Do you feel happy, sad, angry, fearful or ashamed? Emotional intelligence causes me to seek to identify where these feelings come from and why they are there. Believe me, life is going to throw a lot of pain at you. My personal trainer told me that when a person goes to the gym to work out, they aren't building up their muscles, they are tearing them down. When you lift weights, you are doing damage to your muscles. The reason your muscles grow is because your body repairs the damage. This makes them bigger. So next time you lift that much weight, you won't get hurt. You lift more weights and your body gets stronger and stronger. It's like that with our emotions too. Once we experience something hard, it tears us down. It really does hurt, doesn't it? We screw up and embarrass ourselves. We lose a job and don't have any money. But honestly, there is nothing bad that can happen to us that won't return a greater blessing if we let it. We will always come out stronger.

The mind

Every action begins with a thought. Jesus said a person's thoughts determine who that person is –

they're that powerful. Thoughts have enormous potential for good or evil in your life. If you don't proactively renew your mind, your thoughts will default to a pattern set by our fallen world. That's why so many people struggle with their thought lives. In our adventure we are to confront unhealthy thoughts such as worry or hatred, or fantasies about pursuits that will only bring harm. To live an adventure, don't let your thoughts control you. Bring them under Christ's control. Experience the freedom He wants you to have. *'Take every thought captive to the obedience of Christ'.*

Don't just let your thoughts influence you; "take them out," examine them. Find the source. Find the direction they will lead you in! How we think is vital. Our thought life needs to line up with God's word (Romans 12:2). Then to live the adventure, we are to respond in faith. Faith is action; it is proactive, not passive. I know I am – who God says I am; not what the world tells me I am. I am an adopted son of God, and this gave God great pleasure (Ephesians1:5). Nothing can separate me from His love (Romans 8:35-9). God has called me for purpose (Ephesians 2:10).

The will

Power of choice. We are confronted every day with a myriad of good and bad choices. The animal kingdom operates out of instinct, but we are created in the image of God. This means we have a self-operated independent will. The essence of temptation is to persuade us to function independently of God. The basis for temptation is to legitimise our own needs far above the needs of others. The issue here is – are you going to get your needs met by the world, the flesh and the devil, or are you going to allow God to meet your needs?

In your adventure, I urge you to grow in and develop emotional health and intelligence. This enables us to face reality. It empowers us to fearlessly examine the big picture of why we do what we do the way we do, learning to understand yourself and your feelings and their triggers, to process and identify them with God and significant others. Emotional health means we are able to name, recognise and manage our own feelings. Going deeper helps us to recognise and acknowledge that all feelings are valid. However, feelings are transient. They are not reliable or consistent. Hence we don't have to act on them; they are just our feelings at that time. What are you feeling? Happy, sad, angry, fearful or ashamed? Where have those feelings come from and why are they there? On any adventure we have feelings, but we are to be led by the Spirit of God, not our feelings. Our values, lifestyle, behaviour and culture are to be formed out of the word of God, not our feelings. Nevertheless we need to understand, develop and grow in emotional health, by:

- Understanding our emotions.
- Initiating and maintaining close and meaningful relationships.
- Breaking free from self-destructive patterns.
- Being aware of how our past impacts our present.
- Developing the capacity to express our thoughts and feelings clearly – both verbally and non-verbally.
- Respecting and loving others without having to change them.
- Asking for what we need, want or prefer clearly, directly and respectfully.
- Accurately self-assessing our strengths, limits and weaknesses and freely sharing them with others.
- Learning the capacity to resolve conflict maturely and negotiate solutions that consider the perspectives of others.
- Distinguishing and appropriately expressing our sexuality and sensuality.
- Grieving well.

Shadows – roots & remedies

Relationship with your past – sometimes an inability to say no reveals roots in our family of origin. It may be an unspoken rule, eg never upset others; When you are sad or mad, keep it inside; you are responsible for keeping your parents happy.

Consequences of ignoring our shadow/emotional health: Denial; minimising; blame (self or others); rationalise; distract; project anger outwards.

Remedy

Ask yourself (get significant others to ask you) – *"What are you feeling? What's going on inside right now?" "Where does that come from?"*

Ask "What's the problem?" *"Have you repented?" "Of what?"* "How is your connection with God? Your spouse?" Find the problem – then you can experience breakthrough.

Four ways to face your shadow
- Identify what you are feeling.
- Identify clearly your heritage, especially spiritual roots.
- Identify negative scripts passed down to you.
- Seek feedback from trustworthy sources.

Note you are more than your shadow (1Corinthians 4:7). Many fall into one of two extremes – shame (I am totally bad; I am no good) or pride – I am fine and have what I want, after all I deserve it (this can lead to addictive behaviour).

WALK OUT OF THE SHADOWS by:

- Taking time to understand what you are feeling – happiness, sadness, fear, shame or anger.
- Developing a healthy awareness of your shadow – your wounds, self-protectiveness and weaknesses and how you are tempted to sin in your unguarded moments.
- When my buttons are pushed – do you have an overreaction? Instead of blaming others, can you settle down and ask *"what from my past may be causing me to react so strongly to this situation or person?"*
- Learn to be honest with yourself and a few significant others about the struggles, doubts and hurts deep beneath the surface of your life.
- Learn to routinely seek out and embrace feedback from other people about how they experience your flaws.
- Learn to take time to ask hard questions of yourself, even when you are fearful where those answers might lead.

- Learn to seek out guidance from mentors and counsellors or other mature believers to help process how your shadow manifests and affects your life.
- Learn to quickly reach out for help when you are overly stressed or engaging in unhealthy or self-destructive behaviour.
- Learn to identify your weaknesses and failures (mixed motives, fear of what others may think, anxiety, anger etc) in your family of origin or personal history.
- Learn to anticipate moments and seasons that might be difficult and learn to ask for support in advance.

LAY NEW FOUNDATIONS/ROOTS

- We need a Godly prophetic foundation on which to build our lives (1 Corinthians 14:3).
- Be Holy (powerful) as He is Holy (1 Peter 1:13-16).
- Prophetic life is based on relationship, not rules or ritual.
- Relationship with God (John 4:24; Romans 8:11-14; Galatians 4:6).
- Relationship with the past.
- Relationship – marriage/singleness.

- Relationship with others.
- Relationship with God – time listening and seeking him and his Kingdom. Love Him with all your being and doing, serving His purposes and will. Success is obedience, not external.

My long-term vision is to see Everyman complete in Christ (Colossians 1:28). What is yours?

To embrace death is the opportunity of a lifetime as we embrace adoption (Ephesians 1:5) love (Romans 8:38) and purpose & destiny (Ephesians 2:10). Also we embrace being 'unpunishable' by receiving unending, unfailing grace. He is Yahweh – always... (good, righteous etc). By embracing death as the opportunity of a lifetime, we live in and from the current reality of eternal and everlasting life, so to live complete in Christ is to see death as the opportunity or adventure of a lifetime.

Relationships are an adventure

Here are three foundations for any relationship – connection; communication; boundaries.

CONNECTION

Connection is always the goal in every relationship.

Without connection, your relationship suffers. Powerful people keep connection as the priority. Valuing connection should be on the top of your list!

COMMUNICATION

Pursuing the goal of understanding will help you progress through ever deeper levels of honesty in order to build true intimacy and trust in relationship and communicate effectively.

BOUNDARIES

Boundaries are a sign of health in relationships. It's commonly believed that boundaries are meant to keep people out, but they actually communicate value for yourself and others, and in turn help keep people in.

Everything that we allow into our minds, hearts and lives; everything we spend our time and money on; all of it has an impact on how we grow or don't grow, emotionally, mentally and spiritually. As the old computer adage reminds us, garbage in, garbage out. Just as we are what we eat physically, we are also what we consume emotionally, mentally and spiritually. If we don't monitor and adjust our diet accordingly, our souls are in danger of absorbing more and more lethal poison. If you want to stay healthy ask the tough questions, detoxify your life and renew your relationship with God and others.

I Am Accepted

I am no longer rejected, unloved or dirty. In Christ I am completely accepted. God says:

- I am God's child. John 1:12
- I am Christ's friend. John 15:15
- I have been justified. Romans 5:1
- I am united with the Lord and I am one spirit with Him. 1 Corinthians 6:17
- I have been bought with a price. I belong to God. 1 Corinthians 6:19ff
- I am a member of Christ's Body. 1 Corinthians 12:27

Live your adventure: explore, discover, enjoy.

Some thoughts for your consideration

Have you ever accepted the world's, the flesh's or the devil's destiny for your life? What did that (does that) look like? You are able to break free of it.

Have you repented by walking into all that God has for you?

Do you understand your emotions and walk in emotional health? How?

Have you recognised any shadows, and how are you handling them? With whom?

What would you say is your God-given destiny? Why? Has it been confirmed by others? How?

What will your God-given destiny look like for you in six months, 12 months and five years' time?

CHAPTER 3
To thine own self be true

To write this book is a scary adventure. What's scary about writing a book which probably no one will ever read? I suppose it would be like having an in-depth conversation with someone but with nobody listening. Yet when I think about it, that is something like the story of my life. Being born with a cleft palate, it often feels that even when I'm talking, no one is understanding. No one may read or listen, but if God says do it, do it anyway. Leadership in God is not always being right or even understood, but love obedience and faith.

My mother taught me this quote, from Shakespeare's Hamlet: "to thine own self be true, and then it must follow as night the day thou canst not be false to any man." This became a lifestyle from a very early age. I am so grateful. It has helped me to live well throughout my life. However, I have also discovered that for me at least, I am easily tempted to subscribe to being independent, defensive and stubborn. So over time God taught me the importance of being teachable. This is the essence of being true to myself.

To live an adventure involves questioning our beliefs and values. Are they still valid in this situation? If not, what will I do about this? I learned to seek accountability from the depth of my being. I learned to challenge myself – why are you holding to this belief or value; is it really valid? I came to really value books which were outside my comfort zone and experience. I could write notes on them, question them, challenge myself and choose to make myself accountable for my beliefs and values. In your adventure, as you explore and discover, are you open to and actively seeking after correction: input, new ideas that challenge you?

I know it sounds weird, but we need a good relationship with self. Who am I? Am I just a chance product of random evolution? Am I a tiny bunch of atoms in a vast, endless universe? Am I a machine for DNA to reproduce itself? Am I a brain that eventually dies and that's all? Who am I? To live the adventure, I need to have on my lips the words I AM A CHILD OF GOD; I AM A JOINT HEIR WITH CHRIST. I AM REDEEMED – bought with a price, and what a price! I AM CHOSEN OF GOD. As explorers and discoverers, we remind people – you are saints, chosen, special, precious, called-out people. In my parlance, *"You are one of the most important and influential people alive today on planet earth"*.

I've had to remind myself (a bit too regularly!) that no one knows it all or gets it right every time. God has called me to walk humbly before Him. This involves being willing to change, grow and be accountable. At times I've experienced crises arising in people's lives. If they are looking to me for help and answers, I've needed to check myself, ask myself, "Why do you believe that? Why are you really making that decision? Is that a value just for you or for everyone? Is this what God's word really says about this event?"

You are an adventurer, a discoverer, an explorer, a "creativist"; be true to yourself. Know what, or more importantly who, truth is. Jesus said, "I am the truth". To know truth is to know Jesus, and to know the Holy Spirit who leads us into all truth. In addition we need to know the Bible as His word is truth. It is His truth that empowers us to live truth and be true to ourselves. With His truth we can live according to true values and have a true north to guide us. We are on a journey, an adventure, so at some point we will need a compass to guide us. To be effective, the compass needs a true north. This enables us to find where we are and how to get to where we are going. To be true to ourselves, we need a truth within us that is greater than ourselves. We need to know who we are – and whose we are!

Being true to yourself is not about being arrogant. It is not saying "I'm right, so do it". It is saying "I am open to learning and growing, but unless I'm fully persuaded of something else I will be true to myself and what I know of God", at the same time acknowledging that growth and change are here to stay.

Medieval cartographers sketched *"hic sunt dragones"* ("here be dragons") on the edges of their maps. Yet maps of that era often held another image – Christ. The Psalter map (c.1250) was so called because it accompanied a copy of the Book of Psalms. It featured dragons on the bottom, as well as Jesus and the angels at the top. Such a map reminds us of the availability of "true north" as followers of Christ. Yes, there be dragons. But there is also Jesus and the angels. We can follow Him and find our way, as long as we remain true to ourselves in Him. Don't be intimidated by the dragons. Live an adventure. Being true to ourselves is very freeing for any adventurer. Many times I have experienced difficulties with situations or decisions. Knowing that I have been true to myself empowers me to experience peace. It doesn't necessarily mean I was right! However, if I was wrong I can apologise. The freeing aspect is that I can live with myself! Depression and despair cannot gain a foothold if I have been true to myself and to what I believe in God.

The Old Testament and the Gospels focused on the first coming of Jesus the Messiah. We see numerous examples: the obedience of Abraham, the faith of Moses' mother, the faith of the midwives in those times. The courage of David when doing the mundane work of caring for sheep. The way God used the degree of Caesar Augustus to call a census to cause Mary to arrive at Bethlehem at His timing (Luke 2). Living an adventure inspires and influences ourselves and others to see the big picture around us. At the same time we need to be faithful in the detail and application of our lives. Live a life of adventure, discovery and exploration. Being an adventurer in the last days is to be focused on the return of Jesus, the summing up of all things, looking and working expectantly towards all that God will do to fulfil His purposes on the earth. So as a leader or an adventurer, learn to love the work. Anything else is not honouring the process. It's a short cut, which may afford you a few quick wins but won't lead to long-term success. God is more concerned with the process than the product. We need to be, too.

I had a great job, a wonderful wife, a lovely home, but what I was doing had no eternal benefit. You can't just turn values, beliefs, honour or life on and off like a tap. As I grew, and particularly when I took any form of responsibility, I realised how important this value of being true to yourself was. It impacted directly on how I lived my life, the decisions I took and how I outworked my leadership.

For instance, as a young lad I started playing cricket for my local town second team. Because of a shortage of umpires it became recognised procedure that once batsmen were out, they would umpire. This particular day we were playing at a local pitch and had been joined by one of the first team fast bowlers. He was playing for us to regain his fitness after an accident. Nevertheless he had the 'aura' of a first-team player. Anyway, he happened to be bowling at one point when I was umpiring. All of a sudden he bowled a ball that thudded into the pad of the batsman of the other team.

"Howzzzzzzzzzzatt!" was the screamed shout right in my ear. "Not out" came my firm reply. Muttering and glaring, he walked up the wicket to collect the ball. But as he walked past me to bowl his next ball he gently whispered "good decision".

"Be true to yourself" – this doesn't mean you won't make mistakes, but when you do you will be able to sleep peacefully and live contentedly with yourself. When you are wrong, never be afraid to apologise. Over the years on a few occasions I have had to stand before the whole church and acknowledge I got it wrong. The wonderful thing is that people respond to your honesty more than your 'perfection'! I have always held to the advice I was given when apologising: "always apologise within the arena in which you made the mistake". In other words, if I make an error dealing with someone on a one-to-one, that is where I apologise. If I make the mistake before the whole church, then that's where I apologise.

"You are wrong. You need to change your decision." This thirty-minute tirade came from a so-called 'apostolic leader'. He was lambasting me about a difficult action and decision. It was a decision I had reluctantly felt compelled to make in good faith from all I knew at that time. As the tirade continued I finally managed to get a word in: "Just for a minute, would you like to hear my thoughts on this?" I said. "No," came the 'apostolic' reply. "just change your mind and admit your mistake". "Sorry" I said, "you have said nothing to show me my error". I put the phone down. It was one of the hardest actions I have ever had to take in my leadership. Many, many people did not understand. I could not explain, as the issues were very personal for the people concerned. It was not my job to defend my situation, nor to besmirch the reputation of others. I just had to stand, "having done all, stand" or as I said earlier, be true to myself and to what I believed God was revealing to me at that time.

It was a terrible time and many, many people deserted my leadership. I received many hard and painful handwritten letters about myself, but I managed by the grace of God to stay true to myself and not seek to defend myself in the face of accusations. If the apostolic figure had chosen to overrule my decision and take responsibility for it, I would gladly have stepped aside, accepted it and willingly submitted. However that was never the case. Interestingly.

Submit, but if you are left with the responsibility, be true to yourself and God. If in time you are proved to be wrong, then humbly and openly acknowledge your error and ask for forgiveness. To this day, no one else knows from my lips what it was all about. However, I know I have been true to myself. It is not about being right or wrong, but being true. God is my defender, not me! At other times I have got decisions wrong or made a bad action and apologised to the whole church. We are not called to be perfect, but we do need to be "true" and not give up. Live your adventure. We successfully explore by keeping our eyes on the end goal; not the sights along the way.

Years after this so sad and very painful event,

another leader suddenly made it clear he wanted to be the main leader. I had no desire to fight for position, so I chose to walk away. Various things seemed to come together, so I resigned my leadership, put my house on the market and planned to move to another area completely. While this was in progress a friend from another nation phoned to ask what had happened in a situation that the other leader had been asked to resolve. To cut a long story short I had to retract my resignation, take my house off the market and resolve the situation.

For many years I continued to lead the church afterwards. *"To thine own self be true."* Because life is an adventure it doesn't necessarily mean it will be easy. It does mean we will constantly be discovering new things about ourselves and others and the decisions we make.

In all forms of adventures and leadership there are constant challenges to bend, buckle and give up. Don't live merely for security now or money, or anything that doesn't go beyond this life. Can leadership be taught? No, but it can be learned. It is not the teaching that is the essential element; it is the response. A responsive leader creates responsive followers.

As a postscript to the story of the tirade above, when I retired from church leadership I spoke to a local leader who had become involved later in the situation. He said to me in effect that if I hadn't stood at that time he feared for where the church in the town would be now. Praise God. He is the one who builds his church, and to Him is all the glory. In any adventure or form of leadership, storms will come. All of us face storms, and they will be different for each person. Know and understand your areas of vulnerability. What we build on determines whether we stand in the face of storms. When you squeeze an orange, orange juice comes out. What comes out of you when the storms of life squeeze you? Will you continue to push forward in your exploration and discovery of yourself others and God? Adam and Eve faced a storm when the serpent said *"Did God say?"* They chose to not trust God and His word and hence not only did they not finish well but they have made it extremely hard for you and me, their descendants, to lead well but also to finish well.

A commercial flight out of Denver was cancelled and a single gate agent was rebooking a long line of inconvenienced travellers. Suddenly a famous celebrity, who shall remain nameless to protect his ignorance, pushed his way to the front of the line. "I have to be on this next flight and it has to be first class!" he insisted, slapping his ticket down on the counter.

"I'm sorry sir" the agent replied. "I'll be happy to help you, but I have to take care of these folks first."

"Do you have any idea who I am?" he demanded in a loud voice.

The gate agent smiled. She picked up her public-address microphone "May I have your attention please?" she broadcast throughout the terminal. "We have a passenger here who does not know who he is. If anyone can help him find his identity, please come to the gate." As the man retreated, the people in the terminal burst into applause.

So here's my question: Do you know who YOU are?

Never let the "where you are" become the WHO you are. Instead, be true to who you are.

When we are not true to ourselves, we give room for feelings of inadequacy. Inadequacy means we feel we are not good enough, not beautiful enough. We tell ourselves we haven't got what it takes. We've forgotten who we are in Christ. What the enemy means for evil, God can use for good. Being born with a cleft palate made me determined to persevere – sometimes even to be stubborn (sorry). Every time I preached, thoughts came: *they won't understand you! What if there are visitors?* God kept reminding me of His call (not mine) -*"Open your mouth and I will fill it"* (Psalm 81:10). Be powerful – tell yourself God's story. Look in God's mirror, not yours. Being true to who you really are, not what others say you are, will help you to live your adventure. Frequently life exposes people to long-term stressful situations. The urge to act – fight or flight – must be controlled.

Instead of living an adventure, we can often feel overwhelmed by stress when we have both the following dangerous beliefs:

1) a great deal is expected of me
2) I have no control over whether I will perform well.

Live *your* adventure; make *your* discoveries. God has prepared in advance a story for us to live. *You and I are one of the most important and significant people alive today on planet earth.* We are part of an army of ordinary people who carry no worldly weapons yet have within us the greatest power the world has ever known. Live your life, your adventure, your story, founded on the rock of ages. As a disciple, your purpose is to glorify God and leave a legacy for others to grow from. To enjoy their own adventures. To make their own discoveries. Our ceiling becomes others' floor. We can only live one life, but it's never too late to change. Let's build on rock and trust God through all the storms of life.

Ever made a mistake? I have. Ever done or said the wrong thing? I have. What do you feel inside? How do you live? Guilt and a sense of failure seek to condemn and paralyse us. JUSTIFIED means our debts are paid in full by another. (John 19:30). If punishment for your sin has already fallen on Jesus, it cannot also fall on you. So in effect you become no longer 'punishable'. Guilt has been defeated. Your guilt has been paid for in full. So don't let's you or I wallow in guilt.

As an adventurer, identify where you are making faulty assumptions. What are the real issues, problems and challenges? Handle them openly and well. In life there are inevitably multiple challenges. Learn to prioritise the situations, then manage them effectively. Where conflict arises, face it; work through it with honour, value and honesty. Never fail to acknowledge and process the emotions you are experiencing with each event. Remember: know what are you feeling. Why are you feeling that? Where does that feeling root back to? Explore and discover. Learn to identify, address and attend to your emotions with yourself and with others whom you trust.

One day a stranger walked into a shop picked up some bread and milk and made his way to the cash till. "New to town?" the clerk asked.

"Yes" the stranger mumbled, "Just arrived."

The clerk smiled and extended his hand. "Let me be the first to welcome you."

The stranger took his hand reluctantly, frowned and quickly looked down. "So what are the people like in this town?"

"Well... what were they like in the town you lived in last?" the clerk queried.

"Not great" he stammered. "They were cold, aloof and selfish. We were glad to get out of there." He looked up at the clerk.

"I know what you mean," the clerk affirmed. "I'm afraid that's probably what you'll find here too."

To lead and finish well, we need to choose a lifestyle of acceptance One day a stranger walked into a shop, picked up some bread and milk and made his way to the cash till.

"New to town?" the clerk asked.

"Yep. Just moved here with my family," the stranger replied.

"Well then, let me be the first to welcome you," the clerk offered, extending his hand.

"Thanks," the stranger said as he shook it. "Say, what are the people like in this town?"

"Well… what were they like in the town you just left?" the clerk queried?

"Oh, they were fantastic" the stranger replied. "Friendly, upbeat and generous. We hated to leave."

"I know what you mean," the clerk nodded. "I think that's pretty much what you'll find here too."

We get what we expect, so let's understand what story we tell ourselves and learn to tell ourselves a more Godly one. Look in God's mirror (word) not yours!

Some thoughts for your consideration

You are a leader because you influence, for good or otherwise.

Do you accept you are a person of influence – a leader?

Why, or why not?

What will you do about it?

Which book(s) outside your comfort zones or belief systems are you currently engaging with to challenge your beliefs and values?

Who are you accountable to on this?

What does being true to yourself look like to you?

What does it look like to those you are currently leading and mentoring? Can you be fully true to yourself as well and be true to God and His word?

In leadership and in marriage, do you consider being true to yourself vital?

If so, how are you transmitting this to those you are mentoring?

God's ultimate desire for the world is *shalom* (the webbing together of God, humans and all creation in justice, fulfilment and delight). Where can you bring true shalom in a small part of the world?

Practise being true and powerful in every area of your life, big or seemingly insignificant. Aim to get to the point where your security lies within you rather than in people's opinions of you, or even in being right.

Address issues in you and in your leadership team and the situations you lead with kindness, generosity, openness and clarity in order to finish well.

What has spoken to you most in this chapter?

CHAPTER 4

BE HOLY – live powerful

To live your adventure involves exploring, discovering. It is important to be powerful. 1 Peter 1:15-16: *"Be holy as I am Holy"* says God. "Well done" – the accolade of Heaven – is given to those who finish well. Holiness empowers us to not be conformed to the world – it's a way of thinking, culture and beliefs. Being powerfully holy empowers us to resist and overcome sin. Sin represents selfishness, independence and no rebellion. To live a holy and powerful life requires being born again of the Holy Spirit. When we are powerful, we reject independence and live interdependently with Him and others. Being Holy empowers us to reject rebellion and instead live according to God's will and purpose for our lives. Then we equip others to do likewise. I had to recognise that for me this required being accountable to others to ensure I was not just being arrogant. Being holy and powerful requires me to keep a soft heart towards others and live my life as an open book, not being stubborn or proud. Peter obeyed when Jesus said "cast the boat out into the deep." He was a fisherman, Jesus was a carpenter. He had fished all night and caught nothing. "Cast out into the deep and let your nets down on the other side, there are many fish." I wonder, was Peter thinking "Yeah right, who's the fisherman around here?" In obedience, Peter did it; he didn't understand. How could he? But he did it anyway. That is living Holy. It is not about super-spirituality.

Peter demonstrated that adventure is about obedience, not just understanding. It doesn't mean we won't make mistakes, but that we keep going, keep learning, keep growing, keep being changed. Being powerful is about making your choices in God by being true to the Holy Spirit who leads you. The world seeks to make us passive, aggressive or passive/aggressive in our responses to life and situations. Peter made the powerful choice to obey. Everything within Peter was probably shouting, *no! I'm tired! I've been fishing all night! Not again! What's the point? There is nothing out there!* Yet there was a deeper call within him. It called him to do it, saying he would regret it if he didn't. You may not understand, but you need to be true to yourself and your inner voice (the Holy Spirit). Peter chose to be powerful and obey, despite his natural reluctance and doubt. The rest, as they say, is history (for eternity)!

We are called to live powerful lives to be holy; set apart, not controlled. Being holy is about being true to ourselves and to God. True no matter what circumstances or challenges we face. Irrespective of feelings or false news. We are powerful by holding true to our values beliefs and character. We are to inspire and influence ourselves and those we follow and those who follow us.

Jesus warned that in the last days, even the love of the very elect would grow cold. We are to be powerful and proactive, not passive or aggressive. God has a plan. He requires us to step into it by faith, trusting Him both for what we can see and understand and for what we can't. Leadership and life are about being holy powerful; trusting God whatever we feel or experience, trusting and influencing others to trust God to eternity and beyond. Adventurers/leaders do this by seeing and living, holding true to the big picture of the return of Jesus whilst daily living in the detail. In our adventure there are always specific applications to outwork each day. At one time or another most people feel powerless. Good leadership aims to empower them to become a positive influence on themselves and others. Being holy or powerful is about helping people to grow, change and take responsibility for their own actions instead of seeking to place responsibility on to someone else.

It is not about carrot and stick living but empowering those within our sphere of influence to make their own powerful choices. live your adventure. holy living, or empowerment, involves honouring self-control; self-management and self-organisation, all for the common good.

Naturally before we are born again we tend to be either passive, aggressive, passive-aggressive or a mixture of the three. It is only when we are born again of the Holy Spirit that we receive power and can live powerful lives. "Maybe", "possibly", "probably", "basically", "largely" and "hopefully" are all words that smack of indecision and therefore powerlessness. If a manager says to a staff member "Hopefully you'll be okay with this change", his listener might wonder whether she actually has any leeway to challenge it. To live an adventure involves implementing or adopting a plan. Instead of roles being undertaken out of resentment, fear, anger or even duty, the adoption of holy and powerful leadership offers love and purpose to a role.

The Gospel writers are consciously telling the story of how God's one-time action in Jesus the Messiah ushered in a new world order. This declared that a new way of life was not only possible but mandatory for Jesus followers. They were to be a new community, a people who live holy and powerful lives, not powerless victim-focused ones. Rather than blaming others, they were to take responsibility for their lives. Let their yes be yes and their no be no. They were to live "I am" lives, ie from who they were, not from what their experience. They were to be people who loved irrespective of what others did to them; people who said "I will, I do".

To overcome the natural order of behaviour of being either passive, aggressive or passive-aggressive, we are called to be like Jesus and to be "Holy as I am Holy" (1 Peter 1:15-16). Holy is the opposite spirit to unclean, unholy, profane, fearful (1 John 5:19; 2 Timothy 1:7). You cannot be true to yourself unless you are holy set apart.

Be Holy: Love Self – Be Powerful – say "yes I will, I do", or "no".

Be Holy – taking responsible for your life; your behaviour. Character is the willingness to accept responsibility for your own life (this can lead to self-respect).

Be Holy – true to who you are (in God) – loved, chosen, accepted, anointed, called, special.

Be Holy – set good boundaries; (a list of what's OK to do and what's not).

Be Holy – be true to self/God. Give yourself permission to ask for what you need.

Be Holy – refuse to be powerless. Refuse to act like a helpless victim. Don't shame or blame others. Choose life (Deuteronomy 30:19)

Be Holy – love others – so they are free to be themselves around me and so they too are powerful. Encourage them in their boundaries.

Be Holy – practise love over fear.

Be Holy – live in the opposite spirit of the world; which is unclean, unholy, profane and natural under the power of the evil one (1 John 5:19).

Know you are holy/powerful and loved. "I am holy/powerful and loving; I am holy/powerful and loving it!"

Holy Ground – (Exodus 3:5; Joshua 5:15, John 8:12

23, 17:16, Phil.3:20). This involves walking on the earth (which is the Lord's – Exodus 9:29; Psalm 24:1; Isaiah 66:1; Matthew 5:5; in God's way by God's Spirit – living separately from the way the world walks, what the world trusts in and how the world talks. God says "I want you be holy – walk my way! Our holiness can only come from Grace alone through the cross (1 Corinthians 1:30; 2 Corinthians 5:21; Colossians 1:21-2). Holy and powerful people fight from victory, not for victory. Jesus has already won! Jesus' kingdom is not of this world and His followers must not live according to the values and systems of this world.

The values and systems of this world circle around:

Pride of life – which is about control – I am the best (the only one who can……) etc. Lust of the eyes – sees, desires and must have. Lust of the flesh is about appetite and hungers desperately for it. They all ultimately lead to addictive behaviour.

An addiction is an activity or substance we repeatedly crave to experience and for which we are willing if necessary to pay a price (or negative consequence). Examples are addiction, both substance addictions (alcohol, cigarettes, food street drugs etc) and activity addictions (gambling, impulsive sexual activity, shoplifting, overspending etc).

We tend to use the term "addict" to describe the

person who at least in the eyes of others continues an addictive behaviour long after it may have been clear that the substantial price being paid was not worth the benefit. The individual who has lost career, house, family and friends because of cocaine use but is unwilling to consider stopping is an unfortunate example. Addictive behaviour is about demanding satisfaction, now or as soon as possible, for our cravings, passions and supposed wants.

What is common to both positive and negative addictions and what helps us realise that they are two sides of the same coin is the urge or craving to engage in the addictive behaviour and the satisfaction that is felt when the urge is acted upon. The urge is a state of tension and anticipation that is experienced as a desire for the substance or activity. The urge is also experienced as uncomfortable, perhaps intensely so, especially if it lasts a long time. Because we experience relief when the urge is acted upon, there is an increased likelihood that we will act on it again. Scarcity-minded people come from a comparison-based identity and are threatened by the success of others.

Holiness values risk over success

Celebrate the risk step, not the success! Move from your comfort zone and take a risk. Then take another risk, even if the first failed! Take risks each day that build your sense of self-worth. Live in Holiness/power, not unclean, worldly, eg helplessness, paralysis or depression.

Being Holy/powerful is about taking responsibility. This involves:

Never blaming others for anything.

Never blaming yourself.

Never blaming circumstances, events, places or feelings

"The answer is always 'no' unless you ask." —Aaron Walker

God is not "dealing with" our sin. He is establishing our righteousness! He gave Jesus both as Saviour to bring closure to the old nature and as Redeemer to turn a sin habit into righteous behaviour. Then He gave the Holy Spirit to empower us in the process of being made in His image. God gives us permission to be like Him — to view ourselves as He does. Then to take on that identity. It is only in Him and His power that we can fully experience a powerful adventure.

Powerlessness is evidenced when we are unable or unwilling to set boundaries. I choose to either live a powerless/unholy or powerful/holy life. A powerless life is controlled by the whims and needs of others. It is a life controlled by events or circumstances. Powerless people's needs, wants and desires are not expressed. Their speech is "I'll try; perhaps; maybe; if I can", etc. They tend to blame others or their circumstances – it's not my fault; if they hadn't... or if that hadn't happened... Trying is a regular aspect of powerless vocabulary. It's as though we're giving ourselves an out if it doesn't work out. Unholy or powerless people keep changing their opinions, values and beliefs. They often think in line with what they think others think they ought to think!

John C. Maxwell said: *"If you don't have peace, it isn't because someone took it from you; you gave it away. You cannot always control what happens **to** you, but you can control what happens **in** you."* On any adventure and as leaders we hit moments when we feel helpless. The test is how we react to that feeling. Feelings of powerless can lead to frustration, anger and even violence. Unholy or powerless people live from unholy belief systems: I can't do this. It's too hard for me. It isn't even worth trying. I'm not smart enough. That will never work. However, this is unholy talk! If you say these things, challenge yourself to change.

The marriage between me and Linda has not been easy or perfect; it was commitment, realising that for us divorce was not an option, that carried us through. I think commitment, ie holiness, choosing to be powerful, is vital in every area of life – marriage, parenting, discipleship, work etc. Imagine if I said to Linda "I'm going to try to love you." What she wants to hear is "I love you. I'm committed to loving you." That's more than words. That has to be actions. Trying doesn't work!

Is this what God means when He says "Do not be unequally yoked"? Eg, if you are powerful, don't be joined to a powerless person, because if you are, you will always have to take responsibility for them. This will greatly hinder your intention to lead and finish well.

Being holy means we each take responsibility for our own lives. Holy people need to marry and be joined to holy, ie powerful people. Genesis 2:24 is 1+1 = 1 not 1/2 + 1/2!

Never make your wife/husband/children/staff/neighbours feel powerless. Instead always install hope (Hebrews 6:19; 10:23; Proverbs 29:18).

What does Holiness look like?

God revealed Himself to Moses as Yahweh (Exodus 3:14) – I am who I am, eg I am *always* good; *always* faithful; *always* love; *always* a saviour; *always* a healer (Hebrews 13:8; John 8:24; Rev. 1:8). There is self-existence or holiness in Yahweh. Everything owes its life or meaning to God. God is not affected by good or evil, He just is. He is *always*; He is Holy – unmovable, unchangeable. He does not have any unmet needs or desires. He is not co-dependent. Biblically, holiness is not moral perfectionism. It is about constancy, truth, faithfulness and being unmoved by circumstances events or feelings. Holiness means you are led by a passionate vision and are not passive - John 3:16; Philippians 2:3-8; Genesis12:3. Live for the common good (Colossians 1:28).

Scriptures says be holy as He is holy (1Peter 1:13-16). We have to commit. This is what makes the difference. Jesus was holy, He was willing to commit. Even in the face of uncertainty, even when he felt fear when he was not sure he had what it took (Matthew 26:36-44). Jesus put a stake in the ground: "This is what I'm going to do" – commitment. I think part of the issue is that people have this tremendous fear of failure and commitment (1 Peter 2:9; Exodus 19:5-6; Deuteronomy 7:6). Be Holy – powerful people refuse to disqualify themselves (Exodus 4:10; Jeremiah 1:6; Psalm 81:10). Holy/powerful people say words like – yes or no; I will; I can't; I do; I am, or I am not able to. Powerful, holy people are brave enough to say No. Be powerful, be the same irrespective of circumstances, events or feelings – be steady. Be consistent with words and lifestyle – **always**. Ensure that what you say and do line up. There is mystery in God and who He is (John 4:23-4; 17:3). Relationship requires us to keep growing in our knowledge of who He is. He calls us to seek Him (Jeremiah 29:13; Matthew 7:7). Jesus said "follow me", or literally "keep following me"! Find out who you are and what you are like (Isaiah 55:6; Hebrews 11:6; John 17:3).

Life is an adventure. Following Jesus changed the disciples' lives; they became holy, powerful, world changers. They turned their world right side up! This is our call too.

Passive people, powerless people and passive-aggressive people will never live an adventure. Passive-aggressive people are frequently sarcastic. They tease others cruelly or put them down, either directly or behind their backs. They then cover themselves by saying "just kidding". They respond to conflict by shutting others out and giving them the "silent treatment" rather than addressing issues head on.

Passive-aggressive people express their negative feelings harmfully but indirectly. Instead of dealing with issues, they behave in ways that veil their hostility and mask their discontent.

Thoughts for your consideration

What does being holy look like to you? Why?

Do those you lead/mentor understand how to live holy and what it looks like for them?

How important is it for you to finish well?

Are you aware of times or situations in your life where you have reacted in passivity or aggression, or have adopted a passive/aggressive stance?

What will you do to rectify that and ensure that you live powerfully and holy from now on?

How can you equip those you lead/mentor not to react in passivity, aggression or passive / aggressiveness?

What does it mean to you to live and speak in the opposite spirit to the world?

What does this look like in your day-to-day living? What about those you mentor?

To lead and finish well – apply this to your life as a leader. It's important to be aware of the signs of passive aggression. If you realise that you engage in these behaviours, step back and try to figure out why. Then take immediate steps to correct it. After all, your team members likely look to you as a role model for how to act in the workplace. For example, if you have difficulty confronting your team about problems you might want to consider taking an assertiveness course.

What has spoken to you most in this chapter?

CHAPTER 5

Accountability and Team

It is said that power corrupts and absolute power corrupts absolutely. To live an adventure to the full involves teamwork. There is no 'I' in team! We need one another. You can do more together than you can apart. *"Leadership is a relationship in which one person seeks to influence the thoughts, behaviours, beliefs or values of another person"* – Walter C. Wright.

Living your adventure means you always need a team. None of us can, or should, rely purely on our own strength, ability, skill or experience. Being in a team requires us to live authentic lives with each other and living an honouring lifestyle.

Instead of making it all about 'me and my gifting' or 'me looking good', our adventure and hence our leadership should be about valuing, supporting, encouraging and releasing others. If they look good, that reflects well on you. A team means understanding and enhancing the values, gifts and strengths of those around you. It enables the adventure to be lived and outworked. Being in a team is a mentality, not just a fact. With a common mentality we work together for the common good, empowering each other and learning and growing together.

Live your adventure; be accountable. Be authentic. Authentic people own their own mistakes - they do not act powerless. Powerful people openly and honestly confess their errors. Your adventure is enhanced when instead of being independent, self-reliant and self-protective you are interdependent and looking to finish well, not merely trying to survive the current crisis. A team can come in many shapes and sizes, but it is vital that at the core of what we believe and do, there is genuine openness and honesty and the willingness to challenge and be challenged. A team involves open, honest, real loving and kind communication. Be clear about issues and challenges so that each member and part of the team can be heard without fear or favour. We can do more together than we can apart.

However, this inevitably calls us to embrace the reality of conflict and make it positive, not fearful. In any situation where there is more than one person, making a decision is liable to involve conflict, and sometimes conflict occurs even if you are the only person involved in the decision!

Do not be afraid of conflict. Do not make it your goal, but recognise it as a means for your growth and the success of your adventure. Conflict is not negative; as we are roped together we can climb higher and more effectively than on our own.

Be willing to have courageous conversations

Alan Mulally, talking about the car company Ford's turnaround and his journey, said the most important part of the process was when his executive team started being comfortable telling him the truth. In that case it was the truth about what was going on in the business. Mulally had a weekly meeting which he called the Business Process Review, where his team would come in and give him reports on all their metrics. They were losing $17 billion and everyone came in with 'green' metrics week after week. He was able to instill that culture of truth-telling. It wasn't easy. It wasn't overnight. But when they got there, that's when the turnaround had begun. Accountability involves being able to tell the whole truth.

Be clear about the reason for the conversation and the desired outcome. Most courageous conversations falter because there is a lack of clarity about the real issue. Get to the root cause of the problem and address this, rather than focusing on the symptoms.

Cultivate an attitude of discovery and curiosity. Pretend you don't know anything and learn as much as you can about the other person's point of view. Watch their body language and listen to what they are not saying as well as what they are saying. Don't interrupt except to clarify, and let the person talk until they are finished. Then make sure that you have heard and understood everything that has been said by repeating back to them what you think they said. This will ensure the other person feels they have been listened to. Then share with them how you see things from your perspective. Help them see your position without undermining theirs. Seek clarity on how they came to their conclusion and how it differs from your own stance.

Now you both understand each other's point of view, it's time to co-create a solution. Brainstorm and come up with ideas that you both think might work. Find something the other person says that resonates with the solution you desire, and build on this. If the conversation at any time becomes adversarial, go back to inquiry and further clarification on their point of view. The more the other person feels listened to, the more they will engage in co-creating a solution with you.

Without a team we have only one opinion, and therefore by definition it has to be right. With a team we may have a myriad of opinions, but one heart, one mind and one vision to enjoy our adventure.

In any good team there will be open discussions, agreements and disagreements as we seek to find the way of God. This is why accountability is so important. We will not be truly effective as a team unless each one of us is truly accountable; not just to God but to one another, and to others outside of our sphere, including books and teachings.

I urge you for a great adventure to seek first God's Kingdom and His righteousness. Accountability assists us in this process. God is more interested in the process than the product. Accountability will help us in these fast-changing times with the outburst of technological change to social media.

Soon driverless cars will be normal, and rapid change will impact many currently unforeseen areas of life. One idea being mooted is that there will be very few car accidents. That will have implications on the kind of injuries and hence the doctors needed. If a driverless care does crash, how will you assign responsibility? As you live your adventure, be aware of the massive impact of social media and possible intimidation on your journey. Everyone has an opinion, but with social media no one makes themselves accountable. You can say what you like as long as "the powers in power" let you. Condemnation could become rife and conviction rejected.

To live your adventure to the full, don't let your past hold your future hostage!

"Dance like no one is watching. Sing like no one is listening. Love like you've never been hurt and live like it's heaven on earth." – Mark Twain

"No man is fit to command another that cannot command himself." – William Penn

When a person relies purely on themselves they can become dangerous as adventurers and/or leaders.

"The only person you are destined to become is the person you decide to be." – Ralph Waldo Emerson. Avoid the single-minded danger that Abraham Maslow observed: *"He that is good with a hammer tends to think everything is a nail!"*

True Godly submission and accountability are based on wholehearted agreement. They come from the heart of the person who chooses to submit or be accountable. They are not imposed by some hierarchy. True submission is not blind obedience; it is a powerful holy choice and decision. When Jesus said in the Garden, *"Your will, not my will be done"* (Luke 22:42), he was not speaking from powerlessness. He was declaring powerfully. Remember Jesus not only knew the plan He had powerfully set it in motion before the foundation of the world (Revelation 13:8; 1 Peter 1:20; Ephesians 1:4). Jesus had planned for this time. He chose not to let His emotions and fears make him powerless, but powerfully trusted fully in the Father. He actively chose to fulfil His adventure.

During my apprenticeship for leadership, one of the many things God taught me was a vital lesson of obedience and waiting on Him. One particular Sunday I was really confident I had a clear prophetic word to bring to a church in Corfe Mullen. Throughout the service I felt hot and on edge, yet at the same time I kept sensing that God was telling me to wait. This went on right through the service. Confused, I sought God as to what all this was about. I felt Him say He was looking for obedience above all. The following Sunday I felt exactly the same word and felt God release me to share it at the very start of the meeting, and it proved to be significant. Praise God. As God's word puts it, *"obedience is better than sacrifice"* (1 Samuel 15:22-23). For me to live my adventure, I am called to powerful submission and accountability to the Father out of a deep and personal relationship with Him. As Jesus puts it in John 17:3, eternal life, or eternity and beyond, are about knowing personally and intimately the Father and the Son and trusting them and their heart of goodness, irrespective of circumstances or situations.

Adventure, leadership and accountability require listening – listening with your heart, listening because you want to hear, listening with empathy and compassion. Not merely listening till you can find a way into the conversation to tell your story. Not listening to gain an advantage which you can use later, but listening because you care. Listen with openness and honesty and listen to God at the same time.

Be led by the Spirit. When you ask people "How are you?" the answer 95 percent of the time will be "I'm fine". When you ask again, the answer may well be "well, OK". But if you ask a third time you are likely to get the response "well, if you really want to know..." Leadership and accountability require us to listen from the heart, and offer life.

To be a leader requires being willingly and cheerfully able to follow others. Major church leadership really began for me in 1983 when we planted a church in Parkstone, Poole, with five adults and two children (ours). Over the next eighteen months we grew to fifty people. At this time the man who was the key leader was a gifted evangelist and a charismatic guy, and I supported him. Often he would ask me to prepare a word to preach the following

Sunday, but time after time on that given Sunday he would decide he needed to share the word. God was teaching me wholehearted submission and patience.

Around 1985 we joined with Corfe Mullen and Oakdale to form New Life Christian Fellowship. This later was called City Church. However, for various reasons things went wrong and in 1990, with a mixture of joy and heartache, the work was renamed the Vine Christian Fellowship. In 1998, after three years of "courtship", we became formally part of New Frontiers. We have greatly benefited from their shared values, vision, support and friendship over the years. After a while a vision for Poole Revival came to be, and another adventure began. It still continues, and has brought about genuine friendship, honouring and valuing amongst church leaders and enabled churches to work together in Poole in previously unforeseen ways.

Honour calls us to be accountable, to act responsibly and to confront the set of values we believe in and live by (or literally die by) eternally. The wisdom of God is a stumbling block to the Jews and foolishness to the Gentiles. As adventurers and believers, we 'adopt' our own Gods'/Heavens' perspective or what is honourable, good, holy and worthy of living by (Philippians 4:8). Why do I think this is so important for the local church? Well, as Bill Hybels says, the church is the hope of the world. In addition, for the last thirty-five or more years I have always carried in my heart the phrase, "it must work (outwork) in the local church". If we want to grow, to really be a community of God's people living an adventure, we have to show that there is a difference between us. We are a community of blood-bought people on a journey and adventure towards blessing and abundance.

Adventures and leaders need to live; "you don't need to ask permission to take responsibility." Leadership is about influence and seeks to develop leaders who lead with integrity, which is essential to developing healthy organisations, businesses and communities in the twenty-first century. Adventurers and leaders lead not just from the mind but with and touching the heart to ensure the adventure is fully lived. Acceptance of one another in place of competing brings true contentment. Instead of settling for me, we bless others, declaring their amazingness and drawing them into the upward call of God in Christ Jesus. This is where the heart or spirit of a growth mentality comes from. I *am* enough. However, because I am enough, I want to be continually led by the Spirit and be transformed into the image of Christ.

Adventurers and leaders always face the challenge of being right. However no one is always right, and to make mistakes is normal. To live your adventure, refuse the stress of trying to be perfect in an imperfect world. Accountability helps us to test our heart struggles and trust.

In the Kingdom, accountability is not top down, unlike the world. Kingdom accountability says you want to be discipled (Matthew 28:18-20). I therefore ask you to speak into my life as appropriate and relevant – my ministry; my marriage; my relationships; my finances.

So Kingdom accountability is about freely connecting with and submitting to those who oversee us. Overseeing is not hierarchical; rather it is relational. It empowers the adventure.

Connection, growth and discipleship are about being powerful together. They are not about being defensive, passive or aggressive or passive/aggressive. I hope this helps. At least it's how I see it. General George Patton, an American general in the Second World War, once said, *"Once in Sicily I told a general who was somewhat reluctant to attack that I had perfect confidence in him. To show it, I went home. Never tell people what to do and they will surprise you with their ingenuity"*.

Live your adventure. Those who manage themselves empower themselves. They ask questions of themselves and then of others and encourage others to ask them:

- Do you face the consequences of your actions?
- If it goes wrong, do you apologise?
- Or do you blame others, circumstances, events or the past?
- Are you able to take responsibilities without blaming others?
- What does this look like?
- If you make mistakes, what happens?
- Do you desire and seek accountability? in specific areas of ministry? in every area of your life?
- How is that manifested?
- Who are you accountable to? For what parts?
- Are they competent and powerful enough to truly hold you accountable?

Accountability which is only to those who are part of your team or staff is always going to be dangerous. If you are the leader, what would it take for someone to ask you some really hard questions about your life, actions, decisions or moral judgements?

Accountability, by its very nature, requires people who can be friends, yet detached from the day-to-day situations you are involved in and trustworthy enough for you to welcome their deep and hard questions. They should also be people who both your spouse and the other members of the team can have direct access to without seeking your approval. Accountability, remember, is not about trying to trip you up but to finish well.

Here is that famous poem 'If' by Rudyard Kipling. It has been a great help to me as I have sought to lead and finish well. I hope it encourages you.

If you can keep your head when all about you
Are losing theirs and blaming it on you
If you can trust yourself when all men doubt you
But make allowance for their doubting too;
If you can wait and not be tired by waiting
Or being lied about, don't deal in lies
Or being hated, don't give way to hating
And yet don't look too good nor talk too wise:
If you can dream – and not make dreams your master
If you can think – and not make thoughts your aim;
If you can meet with Triumph and Disaster
And treat those two impostors just the same;
If you can bear to hear the truth you've spoken
Twisted by knaves to make a trap for fools
Or watch the things you gave your life to broken
And stoop and build 'em up with worn-out tools:
If you can make one heap of all your winnings
And risk it all on one turn of pitch-and-toss
And lose and start again at your beginnings
And never breath a word about your loss;
If you can force your heart and nerve and sinew
To serve your turn long after they are gone

And so hold on when there is nothing in you
Except the Will which says to them: "Hold on!"
If you can talk with crowds and keep your virtue
Or walk with kings – nor lose the common touch
If neither foes nor loving friends can hurt you
If all men count with you but none too much;
If you can fill the unforgiving minute
With sixty seconds' worth of distance run
Yours is the Earth and everything that's in it
And – which is more – you'll be a Man, my son!

Some thoughts for your consideration

In your own words, what does accountability mean to you?

How do those you lead/mentor understand and live out accountability?

Are your experiences of accountability good or negative? Why?

Is the experience of those you lead/mentor good or negative? How? Why?

How can you make your and others' experience of accountability positive?

> What is accountability?
> I will seek to be honest and review:

a) Positive accomplishments
b) Negative results
c) My strengths
d) Growths
e) My weaknesses
f) Disappointments
g) I will:
h) Evaluate the growth and progress of those I am directly responsible for
i) Outline what I am doing for my personal growth and renewal
j) Highlight the key objectives for the year ahead.

This will take the form of a 5-10 page self-assessment of my contribution to the local church, which will then be sent to others – for instance my fellow Elders, who will review my performance. In addition, I will discuss and review over a day with specific appropriate people.

NB: Consolidate what you have learned so far in this book (and your life) by reviewing it with people you trust and reinforcing it in your day-to-day living, seeking to lead and finish well.

Can you have courageous conversations with others who initially disagree with you?

Have you a heart vision to build a team?

What has spoken to you most in this chapter?

CHAPTER 6

Never give up

"To be a person is to have a story to tell" (Isak Dinesen). People don't want more information – they are up to their eyes with information. They want faith. Faith in you, your goals, your success, your story, your adventure. Facts do not give birth to faith. Faith needs a story to sustain it. Story is a vital and dynamic medium for everyone to express and empowers them to understand themselves and others. Hence I am sharing my story to encourage you in your adventure.

As I mentioned earlier, my start in life was

inauspicious. Nevertheless, it has been a great adventure; and it's not over yet. In fact, I believe the best is yet to come! My inauspicious start emanated from being born with a cleft palate. Somehow, without fully realising it, I chose an adventure. I just about managed to choose life. *"The teaching of the wise is a fountain of life to turn aside from the snares of death"* (Proverbs 13:14). **As you read my story, remember that you too are called as an explorer, a discoverer, an adventurer, a "creativist".**

Around the age of ten I nearly died of pneumonia, even having the last rites read over me. On a lighter note, I failed my eleven plus. I tried to learn to swim, but couldn't. God has empowered me to overcome and He regularly enables me to preach and speak to people. I still find it difficult with people I don't know, but the echo in my ear is *"never give up, I love you"*. He has put eternity in my heart (Ecclesiastes 3:11). On August 1st 1914 Sir Ernest Shackleton (1874-1922) and his crew set sail from London aboard the ship *Endurance*. They were bound for Antarctica, where the famous explorer hoped to traverse the continent on foot. But Shackleton never made the trek, because before the Endurance could reach land, the ship became hopelessly lodged in the ice pack. It was January 1915, and from this point their goal became survival.

The crew faced many hardships in the months that followed, including freezing temperatures and near starvation. The sailors grew uneasy as winter set in and light began to fade. The sun disappeared altogether, not to be seen again until late July. Only those who have experienced it can fully appreciate what it means to be without the sun day after day, week after week; it has driven some men mad. Nevertheless Shackleton inspired his men not to give up and eventually all returned home.

Never giving up is a powerful choice. It empowers you to finish well in your adventure. *"Success is not final, failure is not fatal; it is the courage to continue that counts,"* said Sir Winston Churchill. Leaders inspire rather than require. When faced with a challenge, get smarter! As you get smarter and grow, you lead well and finish well.

From my experience, the urge to give up comes regularly to an adventurer and a leader. It always feels easier to give up when the going gets tough. It feels easier to surrender than to fight; to succumb instead of resisting. However, never give up. This is not about being stubborn or being unable to change and grow. It's about not giving up just because it feels hard. Before the expedition to the Antarctic, it is said Shackleton placed the following advertisement: *"Men wanted for hazardous journey. Low wages, bitter cold, long hours of complete darkness. Safe return doubtful. Honour and recognition in event of success.*" The advert called for people who would be survivors, not people seeking recognition or honour. "*Whether you think you can or you think you can't, you're right*" -Henry Ford.

Don't live worrying about what others think; God is your Father and the Holy Spirit is your guide. He empowers us to never give up and to live our adventure. Know you are loved for who you are; nothing can change that. I have also had to learn that it is not all about me. I am not my own saviour – Jesus is my saviour.

I am saved by grace – undeserved, unmerited, unearned favour. His death on the cross saved me and continues to save me. For myself, I must not give up, but I do surrender to Jesus as my Lord and my saviour. Pain and sickness have come, disappointments regularly occur, but I will not give up, and I encourage you not to; keep focused on living your adventure. I have a Father who delights in me and thinks I am special, no matter what. That's why my relationship with Him is so important to me. It is relationship with Him that inspires me to live this adventure.

I remember the furore that resulted from a trip I undertook on behalf of the church to Japan. It had been reported back, correctly, that I had removed my shoes to enter a Buddhist/Shinto temple. Many folks therefore reasoned (incorrectly) that I had offered worship to idols. The reality was far different. I had felt prompted by the Holy Spirit to enter the temple and declare at each idol that Jesus is Lord. However many people decided to leave the church I was leading on what had been reported to them before speaking to me. It is so important to never give up.

The reality of the significance of this temple 'adventure' was that when I came out of the temple I was confronted by a Monk saying "Who are you? What are you doing here? You are not a believer in Buddha!" Interesting that some who oppose you see something Godly in you, whereas those who are 'on your side' can reject you. Hence the vital lesson – never give up. Live your adventure and finish well.

The Bible says that In these last days many lose "heart" and passion. There is the 'busyness', the 'drivenness' of modern life. It causes many to merely exist and survive. We may feel restless, weary and vulnerable. Modern life has dismantled the "hearts territory" – that of mystery and adventure. Bishop T. D. Jakes tells of his beloved grandmother, who picked cotton. She fought her way through slavery in Mississippi. She earned a degree and finally taught at college. He says she looked beyond the visible – slavery – and rejoiced in the invisible. She looked out of the window and saw far down the road; that's patience, ie "long passion". She refused to give up, no matter what the circumstances told her. I encourage you too to live your adventure.

Here is an extract from an adventure – *The Lord of the Rings*, by J.R.R. Tolkien.

Frodo and Sam are hiking through the mountains on their way to Mount Doom to destroy the One Ring and bring back peace to the land, but at this point all seems lost. They can't see beyond their present reality.

Frodo: *I can't do this Sam.*

Sam: *I know. It's all wrong. By rights we shouldn't even be here. But we are. It's like in the great stories, Mr. Frodo. The ones that really mattered. Full of darkness and danger they were. And sometimes you didn't want to know the end. Because how could the end be happy? How could the world go back to the way it was when so much bad had happened? But in the end it's only a passing thing, this shadow.*

Even darkness must pass. A new day will come. And when the sun shines it will shine out the clearer. Those were the stories that stayed with you. That meant something even if you were too small to understand why. But I think, Mr. Frodo, I do understand. I know now. Folk in those stories had lots of chances of turning back, only they didn't. They kept going. Because they were holding on to something.

Frodo: *What are we holding onto, Sam?*

Sam: *That there's some good in this world, Mr. Frodo… and it's worth fighting for.*

Live your adventure. *"There is some good in this world, and it's worth fighting for!"*

Have you ever watched a sporting event and seen the stunned look on the face of an athlete whom everyone expected to win but didn't? Even smart people can fall into the trap of seeing failure as the end of the world. Frequent success creates expectations that make failure hard to tolerate. People who have to work hard for what they achieve have plenty of practice learning how to deal with failure. They learn to embrace it, because they know that failure is just a stepping stone to success in their adventure. When things come really easy to you, it's possible to see hard work as a negative (a sign that you don't have what it takes). When smart people can't complete something without a tremendous amount of effort, they tend to feel frustrated and embarrassed. This leads them to make the false assumption that if they can't do something easily, there's something wrong with them. As a result, smart people tend to move on to something else, something that affirms their sense of worth before they've put in the time to develop the grit they need to succeed at the highest possible level.

I remember learning to ride a bike, learning to swim, and even more significant, learning to speak publicly when people would either laugh or walk away. Having a defect in any area of life is never easy, but then again, none of us can be brilliant at everything. But we can refuse to give up. In order to never give up, adopt an overcoming mentality. You can be certain that any adventure will always face obstacles.

Learn to overcome. When you experience an obstacle, ask God, and yourself – what is the obstacle intended for? What is its purpose? How will it help you finish your adventure well? Ask God and others – what can be released to you in the examination of this latest challenge? To successfully live an adventure, we all need to learn to fail successfully. If you never fail, you haven't really taken a risk. The word 'risk' means to "place something valued in a position or situation where it can be damaged lost or exposed to danger." Oftentimes, to step into greater levels of our adventure we must be willing to take risks and make mistakes.

How do we cultivate not becoming risk averse? If we want to encourage others into living an adventure, we need to develop a culture where trying and failing is viewed as success. A person who never made a mistake never made anything. Mistakes will happen no matter how great a person you are. The key is never to be defined by those errors.

"The most important thing in life is not to capitalise on your successes – any fool can do that. The really important thing is to profit from your mistakes" (William Bolitho from 'Twelve against the Gods'). To live an adventure and finish well, understand and learn from failure – it is inevitably going to happen, so learn from it! Learn: Failure is not bad. Failure is not something to be ashamed of. Failure is not something to be avoided at all costs! Mistakes aren't necessary evil. Fail early, and fail fast. Failure is like learning to ride a bike or playing a musical instrument – you will make mistakes, but try again. You may learn new ways to do it well.

Growth happens when you put yourself outside your comfort zone.

Failure is a manifestation of learning and exploration. If you aren't experiencing failure, then you are driven by a far worse error – the desire to avoid failure!

What happens when error is discovered? Do people shut down and turn inwards or come together to untangle the causes? The wrong question is, "whose fault is this?" The right question is, "what can I learn from this?" It is never growth to search for a scapegoat.

Celebrate risk over success. In a fear-based culture, people will avoid risk. In a fearless culture people will be willing to explore uncharted and untried areas and ideas and concepts. Each idea, decision or attempt is seen as taking you closer to the desired and best option.

Experiments are to be seen as moving you forward to a better option.

Experiments are fact-finding missions leading towards greater understanding.

"Failure free" is essential in some areas – airlines, hospitals etc – but it is not a goal in other areas. If we neglect our gifts and talents, like an unused muscle they will waste away.

Negative thinking or spiritual warfare seeks to move us away from completeness in Christ and His love to self-reliance, powerlessness and fear. It seeks to move our thinking from why to what. It calls us to seek the "meaning of life" instead of living from our why, ie our purpose (Ephesians 2:10).

"Every child is an artist. The problem is how to remain an artist after he grows up." – Picasso. Every child knows and believes that they are highly creative and can do great things. Children do not approach creativity from the hesitation of disbelief and doubt.

It is no surprise that studies have shown that when asked if they were artists, most children's hands will shoot up in kindergarten, but the number of hands that go up decreases significantly by the time they are in late primary school and then through middle school.

Eventually most of them do not believe that they are artists, and very few hands go up in class.

One important lesson I have had to learn in order not to be defined by my mistakes:

Revelation - Repentance - Renounce - Receive - Resist

Revelation *– (from God)* - Recognise the true nature and cause of the problem, and if possible the sin which gave it access in our lives.

Repent – change direction. Look towards God, not towards sin. No longer believe in the curses placed on you. No longer be bound to the past and other people's words over your life.

Renounce – Break your agreements with it, conscious and unconscious. Break its authority over your thinking, emotions and actions. it no longer belongs to you; it has no more authority in your life. It is not your problem any longer.

Receive – your freedom and liberty through and by the Spirit and the word.

Resist – James 4:7. Don't be passive, but actively and continually resist the lies and tactics of the enemy or the past.

"If a man does not keep pace with his companions, perhaps it's because he hears a different drummer. Let Him stop to the music which he hears, however measured or far away" – Henry Thoreau. Albert Schweitzer said: *'I know not what your destiny will be, but one thing I know: the only ones among you who will be truly happy are those who have sought and found how to serve."*

One day a farmer's donkey fell into a well. The farmer frantically thought what to do as the stricken animal cried out to be rescued. With no obvious solution, the farmer regretfully concluded that as the donkey was old and as the well needed to be filled in anyway, he should give up the idea of rescuing the beast and simply fill in the well. He tried to persuade himself that hopefully the poor animal would not suffer too much.

The farmer asked his neighbours' help, and before long they all began to shovel earth quickly into the well. When the donkey realised what was happening, he wailed and struggled, but then to everyone's relief, the noise stopped. After a while the farmer looked down into the well and was astonished by what he saw. The donkey was still alive and progressing towards the top of the well. He had discovered that by shaking off the dirt instead of letting it cover him, he could keep stepping on top of the earth as the level rose. Soon the donkey was able to step up over the edge of the well and he happily trotted off.

Life tends to shovel dirt on top of each of us from time to time. The trick is to be powerful and shake it off and then take a step up. You may fall down a deep well, but it's where and how well you finish that matters. When you have eternity in your heart and on your mind and look to finish well, mistakes and problems are just part of life; they do not define what your life is about or worth.

When I was baptised, I believe God said to me something that was so difficult for me to hear (*"I the LORD am your God Who brought you up from the land of Egypt; Open your mouth wide and I will fill it"* – Psalm 81:10.) I had to somehow choose life. How could I preach, let alone lead a church? No one would understand me; this is too hard, it is ridiculous, but as Proverbs 14:12 says, "There is a way which seems right to a man, but its end is the way of death." – I had to choose life (ie Jesus).

Even now, when I meet new people and fear not being understood – I have to choose life; I cringe when I hear my voice when I preach; I cringe when I hear an answering machine message I've left for my wife Linda. I struggle with death and its fruit and have to constantly choose life. *"Death is the last weapon of the tyrant; and the point of the resurrection is that death has been defeated." God said trust me and see what I will do – my power is perfected in your weakness.* Every time I preached or even met someone new, I have had, and still have, to refuse to be defined by my weaknesses or problems. The truth is I am loved and chosen as a child of God – holy and powerful in Him.

You and I have a choice today, life or death – **choose life**. I did, and I do, and you can too!

Simon Sinek writes: *"It needs a very special and rare partnership between one who knows WHY and those who know HOW. It is not an accident that these unions of whys and hows often come from families or old friendships."*

Thoughts for your consideration

What situations or circumstances tempt you, or have made you give up?

How do you feel when you give up? How do those you lead/mentor feel when they give up?

What will strengthen your resolve, or that of those you mentor, when faced with difficulties and challenges which make you want to give up?

Have you ever been defined by your mistakes? When? What did it feel like? What did it look like?

What about those you lead/mentor – have you or anyone else they mentor been defined by their mistakes? What did this look like? What changes will you implement to assist them to finish well?

How do you ensure that you will not define yourself or others by their mistakes? What will this look like on a day-to-day basis?

Are you a person and a leader who inspires or requires? Dare you ask those close to you and your fellow leaders/those you mentor which you are – an inspirer or a requirer?

Whatever the response, ask them how this is seen in your life.

What has spoken to you most in this chapter?

CHAPTER 7
Dreams and vision

To live an adventure, understand "*a person without a progressing vision is a person without a future, and a person without a future will always revert to his past*" – Danny Silk.

What difference do you think it would have made to the ten spies, and therefore for the whole nation of Israel, if not only Caleb and Joshua but all of them had a vision for the promised land and what God would do? Numbers 13:25-33; Which group would you have naturally aligned yourself to – the ten or the two? Why? How do you know?

A person with a progressive vision will live a powerful life, proactively looking forward towards eternity and beyond. In his book *Leadership is an Art*, Max Degree says *"the two primary responsibilities of a leader are to point the direction or define reality, and to say thank you!"* To live an adventure, we are called to break barriers to do things that have never been done before. Free people free people! We represent God to this fallen and desperate world.

Dreams without goals are just dreams. Just having a dream will set us up for disappointment. Dreams need goals if they are to be implemented. Goals involve discipline, planning and hard work. Without goals, we are merely dreamers, and we live in the disappointments of unfulfilled dreams. Goals call on us to plan five years, one year, six months, quarterly, monthly and daily. For instance, what three things do you want to achieve in these time scales, starting with the one furthest away? Break these down over the period. Ensure you are reviewing and checking regularly. Test the progress you are making towards those goals. Always aim to do at least three things per day towards them. Even the smallest step can be a step towards progress and fulfilment. Productivity isn't simply about getting more done. It's about getting the right things done with a specific goal in mind. Live your adventure!

Vision is not merely important for your adventure but for those who follow.

The USS *Astoria* was the first U.S. cruiser to engage the Japanese during the battle of Savo Island. A night action was fought on the 8-9th August 1942. Although she scored two hits on the imperial flagship *Chokai,* the *Astoria* was badly damaged and sank shortly after noon on 9th August.

About 0200 hours, a young Midwesterner, Signalman 3rd class Elgin Staples, was swept overboard by the blast when the Astoria's number one eight-inch gun turret exploded. Wounded in both legs by shrapnel and in semi-shock, he was kept alive by a narrow lifebelt which he managed to activate with a simple trigger mechanism. At around 0600 hours, Staples was rescued by a passing destroyer and returned to the *Astoria*, whose captain was attempting to save the cruiser by beaching her. The effort failed and Staples, still wearing the same lifebelt, found himself back in the water. It was lunchtime. Picked up again, this time by the USS *President Jackson*, he was one of 500 survivors of the battle who were evacuated to Noumea.

On board the transport, Staples for the first time closely examined the lifebelt that had served him so well. It had been manufactured by Firestone Tire and Rubber Company of Akron Ohio, and bore a registration number. Given home leave, Staples told his story and asked his mother, who worked for Firestone, about the purpose of the number on the belt. She replied that the company insisted on personal responsibility for the war effort. The number was unique and assigned to one inspector. Staples remembered everything about the lifebelt and quoted the number to her. It was his mother's own personal code and affixed to every item she was responsible for approving! (From Page 48 of *Strange Things Happen at Sea*, by Commander Eric J Berryman). When you can't see, you sometimes need glasses to correct your sight, or binoculars to see into the distance. With vision, never forget the detail.

"Only he who keeps his eye on the far horizon will find the right road" – Dag Hammarskjold.

Without a vision of eternity, we will always work from the here and now. When we focus on the here and now, we are more easily tempted to seek our here and now needs and desires, instead of living our adventure. Albert Einstein said, *"Imagination is more important than knowledge."* Memory is past. It is finite. Vision is future. It is infinite. Vision is greater than history, greater than baggage, greater than wounds of the past. If there is one task almost universally affirmed for a leader or an adventurer, it is casting vision. Not just any vision: if we're taking a hill, we need to define where the hill is and why it is worth taking. "Here's the target on the wall. Here's what we're trying to do." This is the adventure we are undertaking, and these are the reasons.

On a personal level, casting vision is helping individuals see how they are contributing to that vision in ways that expand their own vision. It also values their investment. It's walking up to a person serving in the nursery and saying: "I'm so glad you're serving. Thank you. Because of you there's a young couple in the service able to explore what Christ can mean for their lives. That's what you're doing." We need eternity in our hearts and souls to live powerfully in our day-to-day existence. Otherwise there is a strong temptation to "feed my passions"; "I deserve…"

To live an adventure, we need to live our lives like the first man to step on the moon -*"one small step for a man, one giant step for mankind"*. In other words, I may be doing seemingly small and insignificant things, but by serving with eternity in my heart I can trust God to outwork His purposes far beyond what I can ask or seek.

To live out a vision, remember Stephen Covey's advice: always start with the end in mind. Do first things first and be proactive. However, focusing on something can make it more difficult to see. The goal is to learn to suspend, even if only temporarily, the patterns or habits that obscure your Vision. A vision is like being involved in an exodus, a journey, an adventure (Isaiah 2:2-5). Abraham was told to leave his family (Genesis 12:1-3). It takes vision to obey. Sometimes that vision is of something better; sometimes it's the vision that 'God is good'. Jesus said *"follow me"* (Matthew 4:19-20). It takes vision to obey. The Spirit desires to lead us (Romans 8:14).

Vision calls us to exodus from the world's thinking and mindsets (Romans 12:2) to the Kingdom of God mindset (Matthew 6:33). Our adventure involves moving from control to freedom; from domination to liberty; to embracing true freedom and liberty in the Spirit. (2 Corinthians 3:15-18; Galatians 5:1-2). From law to grace; from despair to hope; from doubt and what ifs to faith; from fear to Love.

As people, whether believers or not, we are created spiritual in nature. We are spiritual conductors, and we create an atmosphere, a spirit if you will, around us. However, we can only reproduce on the outside that which is on the inside. Living from vision empowers us to be open to new opportunities; to creative thinking. Vision prepares us to embrace uncertainty. Vision is a catalyst of creative ideas. When we respond to vision, seek to stay positive; your success is in your attitude. Refuse to be negative. Adopt God's YES mentality (2 Corinthians 1:20). Let your vision grow in terms of astonishment, of amazement, in joy and gladness. Live the adventure by living out of thankfulness not merely looking forward. I am so thankful to my parents for the love and home they gave me growing up. I am so thankful to my brother and his wife for the money they gave us when we got married to enable us to put a deposit on our first home. Abraham was blessed. Blessed means 'spoken well of'. To bless means to celebrate with praises. In other words, when we bless, we say 'you are amazing'. Through Abraham, all the families of the earth were to be declared amazing – not competed with, but praised and valued (Genesis 12:1-3). All the families of the earth are to be brought into the reality and understanding of their uniqueness and blessedness (completeness). I have been so blessed with my wonderful wife and brilliant sons, daughter in law and grandchildren. Also the Family of God who have loved and encouraged me. This is our adventure in my book, an adventure worth living.

Israel was commissioned as God's special and amazing people chosen to bless – declare the amazingness of God and of all the peoples of the earth. The church in Acts had all things in common. They were to live as amazing, unique people delighting in enjoying and sharing each other's amazing attributes – an adventure:

a) Develop and live a culture of honour.

b) Sound the trumpet – When good men do nothing, evil prevails. Live in grace by faith/trust.

c) Without vision, people perish (Proverbs 29:18). Or more literally, they "cast off restraint." Without a vision of God or why we exist, we have no sense of true north, no boundaries, no funnelling of energy, no focus, no knowledge of our identity, purpose or destiny or real sense of adventure.

As God's people we cannot be passive, apathetic or lukewarm. We are called to transform – to be salt and light (Matthew 5:9-16). It appears that as believers we have allowed our voices to be silenced in most, if not every major area of society. For instance we are forbidden to share our faith and often even to talk about God in most areas of society today. We need to understand the times. Look in the face of increasing persecution. We cannot afford to be complacent in the UK. As Martin Luther King Jr. once said, *"We are not the master of the state or the servant of the state but the conscience of the state"*. This is a vital adventure and worth living.

Love without courage and wisdom is sentimentality. Courage without love and wisdom is foolhardiness. Wisdom without love and courage is cowardice. But the one who has love courage and wisdom moves the world.

Only a leader in the adventure can give permission. This isn't about control but the privilege of turning people loose. A leader enables people to develop their gifts, chase ministry dreams, take risks and explore new ventures. The Apostle Paul wrote in the New Testament Letter of Ephesians that the job of a church leader is to equip people for ministry. An adventurer and/or a leader clears the way for people to follow paths of God's design and leading. Going further, a good leader sees things in people and encourages them to explore things they never dreamed of for themselves. So it's not simply permission but provocation. It's putting your arm around someone's shoulders and saying "I see you doing this" or "I think you could make a difference here". "Live the adventure."

Keep a progressing vision. You are never too old to dream. Let your vision dictate your goals. Then seek to implement your goals, to inspire others to own their own vision and set their own goals. The promise is that even old men will dream dreams. I still have dreams to fulfil, for instance:

My dream of forming a question centre

Consider the world view questions: Where did we come from, and who are we? What has gone wrong with the world? What can we do to fix it? How now shall we live?

Reflect on the response to the first and most foundational of these questions – "Where did we come from?" There are a limited number of answers at our disposal: we came about by chance (the naturalist contention); we don't really exist (the Hindu response); or we were spoken into existence by God. Even if one makes more obscure suggestions, such as Cambridge physicist Stephen Hawking, who intimated that we were seeded here by another race of beings from another planet, one would then have to account for *their* existence. So for the Christian, the answer to "Where did we come from and who are we?" gives a foundation for thinking that no other answer gives. Because we were created, there is value in each person. There is meaning and purpose to every life. There is Someone above and outside of our existence who stands over it as authority. This is the power and force of a biblical worldview and how it cuts through the cultural morass of clouded thinking.

The goals of this dream for a Question Centre are:

a) To develop and encourage people to think creativity and for themselves.

b) To ask questions rather than merely accept the status quo.

c) To encourage people to think through the questions of life – Why do I exist? What is life about? Where am I going?

d) To encourage creative thinking to develop new ideas for own businesses or existing ones to create employment.

e) To cause those who feel they "don't fit" and have nothing to offer to see new hope and vision for their lives.

f) To help people find their identity, purpose and destiny.

g) Envision people to live as heroes and not bystanders.

h) To value people and their ideas and encourage creative approaches to life.

I) To encourage fearful or anxious or sidelined people to be re-envisioned and gain confidence and hope to attempt new things.

j) Consider a system of raising finance from individuals who can afford some small investments to provide hope for those who without this investment would be unable to break free of mundane existence and the poverty trap.

k) To provide a 'wow' factor concerning life and the wonders of nature.

l) To educate regarding health and living healthily.

m) To inform regarding environment and safeguarding it.

n) To encourage engagement with the wonder of creation and create a desire to explore further.

MY DREAM of "Theology – So What?"

A dream to make my teaching material easily accessible online and to encourage those who read it to consider the implications for their own lives of each area of teaching. It is intended to be easily accessible and to challenge us as individuals to consider and apply the amazing things we discover when we start to study theology – the knowledge of God. I have a desire to release understanding of God's Father heart by healing our orphan heart, resulting in separation and shame.

My dream of a new generation

WHY? to inspire young and experienced mission leaders to passionately grow in God.

HOW? I need a dedicated creative team of people (possibly 4-7) who are able to work and think "outside the box" and be part of a committed core brainstorming team to produce the first quality production. The first production would be "Releasing people to dream and fulfilling those dreams".

WHO? Looking for technician skills, organisational skills, administration, creative ideas, resources, people, drama, production, photography ideas folks, scriptwriters, film crew directors.

WHAT? To produce a quality production of 8-10 minutes.

If you know of others who might be interested, do let me know – I think for ease of working I want to keep the core team to 7 max, but no reason each team leader can't have many more in his or her team.

My dream of a story-telling centre

Every person is unique.

Every person has a story to tell (perhaps many).

Every person can learn from the story of another.

This dream may perhaps involve working with schoolchildren and old people, in fact anyone and everyone, as we all have a story to tell – though we often don't realise it. Perhaps you are the person with the skills to "tease out" the story hidden within a person young or old or in between.

I have a vision for a film and video centre and an editing suite.

WHY? to encourage storytelling, develop greater unity across the ages and encourage creativity.

Dare to dream

What do you do when you feel intimidated? Perhaps you have a difficult phone call to make, a difficult situation to address. Perhaps you feel out of your depth and anxious about the outcome. A guy phones me and asks me for my support. His wife has already told me he is having an affair. The guy reminds me his is by far the best 'tither' in the church, and I don't doubt he is right. If he leaves, finances could be very difficult for the conceivable future. There are always two sides to a situation. But what do you do? Do you respond to the intimidation and fear, or to the bigger vision which now seems even more impossible?

A big vision requires a world view, but what is a world view? The term is from the German *Weltanschauung* (literally: "world perception"), but the definition goes beyond just a set of ideas by which you judge other ideas. Rather it is as Gene Edward Veith has written: *"a way to engage constructively the whole range of human expression from a Christian perspective."* Or as Jonathan Edwards – arguably the greatest intellect America has ever produced – once contended: the basic goal of any intellect is to work toward *"the consistency and agreement of our ideas with the ideas of God."* It is just such a world view that allows prophetic voices to ring loud and clear, such as

Martin Luther King Jr.'s voice. He penned these immortal words found in his jailhouse correspondence: "*... there are two types of law: just and unjust... A just law is a man-made code that squares with the moral law or the law of God. An unjust law is a code that is out of harmony with the moral law... Any law that uplifts human personality is just. Any law that degrades human personality is unjust. All segregation statutes are unjust, because segregation distorts the soul and damages the personality.*" King's argument was based on the worth of a human being bestowed by God, regardless of what other humans might have to say. King laid claim to a law above man's law. No other world view would have given King the basis for such a claim. From such a world view the world was changed. Hence the call for adventurers.

Remember, for a vision to be outworked never forget the detail. It will help to outwork as follows and in order and regularly review and reference each as relevant.

Identify mission and values.

Set goals.

Plan annual goal(s).

Plan half-yearly goal(s)

Plan monthly goals (aim to accomplish 3 things this month).

Plan weekly goals (aim to achieve 3 things this week).

Plan daily (aim to do at least 3 different things per day).

A vision or an adventure often involves taking small steps, not just big ones.

As a new father and lawyer, John Grisham woke up early every morning, went to his office and wrote a page of his novel. That was his goal. One page per day for 365 days. It took three years, but by the end of that time he had completed the manuscript for his first book, *A Time to Kill*. The book would eventually go on to be a bestseller, the first of many. In the process, Grisham would invent a new genre—the legal thriller. Soon he would become one of the world's most successful authors.

Grisham became a writer by stealing away a little time each day, thirty minutes to an hour a day. That was it. With a growing family and a new career, it would have been reckless to quit law and become a full-time author. In fact that wasn't even his goal; he was just writing to see if he could do it. He took one step at a time and three years later he had a book. It wasn't until he was two bestsellers in to his writing career that he left his law practice to pursue writing full time. The first step to launching a big dream is just that—a step, not a leap. Small changes over time lead to massive transformation. You can do extraordinary things when you are patiently persistent. Learn to live your adventure one step at a time. You and I were born to bring impossibilities down to earth. We have to go through the giants to reach the promised land. It's when you go through a trial you have a testimony. It is when you've had a mess and cleaned it up that you have a message!

To develop vision and a positive outlook for your future:

Ask – why me? Spend 60 seconds at the start of each day- Why are you so blessed? Remind yourself who you are in Christ.

Who cares? The question is meant to tease out our values and mission. It is to be answered with: "I choose to care and I choose to thrive because…" eg, a mission statement could be: "I choose to care and I choose to thrive because God demands it, my family deserves it and the world is starved for it."

At the end of your day, ask "What more can I do to ensure that tomorrow is better than today?" This allows you to form a strategy for tomorrow.

Thoughts for your consideration

What are the visions you are carrying in your heart? Write them down and ask God about them.

Do you know any specific visions of those you lead/mentor?

How does this enhance or conflict with the vision in your heart? What will you do about this?

Have you or others in your leadership team or those you mentor ever given up on a vision? If so, why? Would it be relevant to you or them to consider picking it up again? Why? How?

What giants do you or those in your team or those you mentor face? How can God and you/they overcome them?

Do any of you dreams inspire you (or those you mentor) to either help you or fulfil your own dream? I would love to hear from you either way.

What goals are you implementing to ensure your dreams don't just remain dreams and lead to disappointment?

What practical steps are you acting on to see these goals fulfilled?

What has spoken to you most in this chapter?

CHAPTER 8
The weapon of forgiveness

As my amazing, wonderful and beautiful wife so eloquently put it, *"Forgiveness is a weapon"*. Forgiveness is not passive. Forgiveness is a weapon. A love weapon. Love overcomes all things. Forgiveness frees you from resentment, bitterness, envy and jealousy. Forgiveness is a weapon that empowers you in your adventure. Knowing your identity as an adventurer, discoverer, explorer and creativist, this empowers me to implement and activate the weapon of forgiveness. It reminds me that there is more to my life than me, my feelings and my experiences.

God, from before time as we know it began, had set the weapon of forgiveness into being. The Godhead knew that when they created man he would fall into the clutches of the enemy. Nothing takes God by surprise. He planned an eternal redemption through Jesus, a redemption that would make love, grace and forgiveness weapons empowering mankind to walk in victory and freedom. At the cross, all my sin for all time was forgiven. All my sin, past present and future, was forgiven through the death and resurrection of Jesus. Forever! I am forgiven. I become no longer 'punishable!' (Isaiah 53). 'Unpunishable' is my description of my state now before God forever. There is no more fear of punishment. God is love. Fear's power lies in punishment in one form or another. I am forgiven; that is my weapon to live by. Through God's love and grace by faith, I now have the weapon of forgiveness in my armour. Forgiveness is a weapon against the enemy. The enemy wants to separate us from God and each other. Forgiveness refuses to allow that to happen.

When we feel fear, we should respond in the opposite spirit. We should receive it as an invitation to love. Remind yourself that love overcomes all fear. His love is unconditional. There is nothing I can do to make God love me more. There is nothing I can do to make God love me less. I am loved! The world tries to teach me I am rejected, unloved and unlovable. I have had to continually learn to use forgiveness as a weapon. I am forgiven and loved. To effectively live the adventure, I am learning to use the weapon of forgiveness. This overcomes all the lies of fear and rejection.

God delivered me through His love; He accepted me. He calls me amazing, fulfilled, satisfied, spirit, soul and body with God's and your own amazingness. I no longer live a competitive life but live an amazing one, out of the reality of being completely fulfilled in Christ. *I am God's gift of love to others!* That's the power of the weapon of forgiveness.

God looks at me and says "You are amazing". Instantly, negative thoughts come into my mind with reasons why I am not. The weapon of forgiveness empowers me to agree with what God says – I am, you are, amazing. You and I have an adventure to live. God says He made me in His image AND He has put the same Holy Spirit in you that raised Christ Jesus from the dead. I am amazing because God has made me amazing. When we look at a mountain or a bird or a flower, we may say, "That's amazing, has it done anything itself?" No, it's how it was made. It's the same with us.

Live daily in the weapon of forgiveness. God has

made us amazing. No room for pride, only delight. Don't put yourself down or belittle yourself. The weapon of forgiveness empowers us to forgive our own picture of ourselves and live in God's truth. So we can praise God for what He has made us. We are all different but equal before God. When we say "I am no good" or "I am not amazing", we disagree with God. This belittles His creative gift and stops His power and heaven's resources flowing through us to others. It is a roadblock to our adventure. When we praise God and give Him glory for making us so amazing, we open the door to heaven's resources. We allow them to flow through us for the blessing of others and the nation's, and we live an adventure. This is about who we are, NOT what we do.

Forgiveness is our weapon against all fear. God is love; perfect love casts out all fear. God invites into His love. Whenever we face a fearful situation, we should not focus on the fear but on God and who He is, and that we are forgiven. There are reckoned to be around two thousand classified fears. However psychiatrists say we are born with only two innate fears; the fear of falling and the fear of loud noises. Every other fear is learned. That's good news. because if fear can be learned, it can be unlearned. The only Kingdom or God-ordained fear is the fear of God. 1 John 4:18 shows us the goal of love is fearlessness – being courageous.

The goal of life is not to eliminate fear but to muster the courage to overcome it. Worship is forgetting what's wrong with you and remembering what's right with God. Live the adventure; exercise the weapon of forgiveness.

Good is often the enemy of great. Let me tell you what may be stopping you from stepping out in faith; probably the same things which try and stop me. We almost always second-guess ourself. We make a decision and immediately wonder if it's right. Because God requires a relationship of trust, generally speaking you are never going to be more than eighty percent certain. Be powerful; waiting for greater certainty may cause you to miss an opportunity. You can't experience success without risking failure. One courageous or trusting choice may be the only thing between you and your dream becoming reality. Acting in love, not fear, may be as simple as making a phone call, downloading an application form or sending an email. To live the adventure, we have to push over the first domino. It is small acts of courage that change the course of history. I know that is true for me whenever I choose to fire the weapon of forgiveness. The weapon of forgiveness empowers me to accept myself as God sees me - it enables me to live free from having to prove my worth.

You cannot train a bird of prey with punishment (ie fear of it); you train it with rewards, blessings and encouragement. You give it freedom. Herd animals are trained with control, domination and intimidation. This ensures that each one knows his place in the 'pecking order'. People are individuals. You empower them with honour, respect, blessing their identity, rewards, encouragement and giving them freedom – not freedom to do whatever they like but freedom to live responsibly for the common good. They learn consequences, good and bad, of their actions. Also they learn to exercise the weapon of forgiveness – of themselves and of others. God is love. God is in charge, but not in control – we are free to... We are responsible to... "*They never tell you that when you become a control freak it will cost you a healthy love life. But it's true. You can't control somebody and have intimacy with them at the same time. They may stay because they fear you, but true love casts out all fear.*" so writes Donald Miller in *Scary Close*. Utilising the weapon of forgiveness brings freedom from fear of punishment.

Real love stories don't have dictators; they have powerful participants. True intimacy can seem frightening; it's the one thing we all want, but we must give up control to enjoy it. It is only by being powerful, releasing love and using the weapon of forgiveness that intimacy can flourish. Most of all, I had to learn the weapon of forgiveness towards myself.

Whether on an adventure or in leadership, I have found it easy to slip into fear. Fear of failure, fear of what others think, fear of all different types and sorts. I have constantly to remind myself to use the weapon of forgiveness. I am loved for who I am, not for what I do (at least by God!) Courage is not the absence of fear. Rather it is experiencing fear and doing it anyway. You are an adventurer, a leader; you have to lead yourself through a fallen and sometimes dangerous and difficult world. So ensure you love yourself. See yourself as a 'bird of prey'; reward, honour, value yourself. Be secure in your identity. Never punish yourself – learn, grow, but don't punish yourself or the people you lead.

Powerless people are fearful and thus often attack. Life to many is a game of "king of the hill", and when you stand, someone tries to take you down. That's the herd mentality. But the greatest and most powerful adventurers or leaders, the ones who truly impact the world, are able to forgive and love those who attack them. They use powerful weapons of forgiveness and thus do not seek to or need to impress others.

The Weapon of Forgiveness reminds us we are loved. Love empowers us to take risks and be creative. According to creativity researcher and scholar Sir Ken Robinson: *"We have this extraordinary human power, the power of imagination. We take it totally for granted. This capacity to bring in to mind things that aren't present and on that base is to hypothesise about things that have never been but could be. Every feature of human culture, in my view, is the consequence of this unique capacity."* Fear and condemnation seek to stop us living powerfully and in love.

One amazing day a door opened into my heart and I read a scripture which said: *"Therefore there is now no condemnation for those in Christ Jesus"* (Romans 8:1). God is a God of relationship; He speaks to His children, He desires intimacy and interaction.

As I read this passage I felt it come to me like a conversation – "There is no condemnation for those in Christ Jesus". Are you in a relationship with God – is Jesus Christ your Lord and saviour? Yes? Then there is no condemnation! Yippee! so that means I can go to heaven when I die? Yes, and more.

For who is there no condemnation? Me.

Read it again! When is there no condemnation? It says 'Now'. Good - when is now? Is it just when you die? Well, no... it's now! Suddenly I realised that relationship with God made me free from all condemnation FOREVER! Having been brought up in a Catholic setting, I never felt I could do enough. I had to regularly confess my sins to the priest, but suddenly came this revelation –I have received forgiveness, I am loved. Love means there is no more condemnation for ME!

A few days later I had to work late in Bournemouth. Glancing at my watch, I suddenly became aware of the time. I shut down the office and ran out to my car. I jumped into the car, swung it around and guess what! CRUNCH. Oh no! I looked around. There was only one other car in the car park, and it was a Jaguar. I looked about; there was no one around, no one had seen me, no one knew. Phew! I drove off.

Don't you know that when you are late the traffic lights are always red? I stopped at the lights. I "felt" this voice say to me, "how do you feel?" Fine, I lied.

Sure enough, the next set of traffic lights was also red. Again this voice on the inside said, "how do you feel?" Not brilliant. Yet again red traffic lights –" how do you feel?" came again. "Terrible," I blurted out. "I drove into a car and just drove off. I feel terrible." OK, so what will you do about it? Tomorrow is too late. Tonight I will go and sort it out. But I still feel terrible. Why? It's obvious, isn't it? But don't you know there is no condemnation for those in Christ Jesus? Yes of course. That means I can correct my mistakes, and I am not condemned by them. I enjoy and delight in my relationship with Jesus.

That day changed my life, and it could change yours. Forgiveness is a weapon; make sure you use it. It works for you as well as for others.

The sun doesn't need to turn up its juice or search for more light. In fact it doesn't need to do anything; it just is. Love is a kind of light. Love doesn't seek more love or doubt itself. We are both children of light and love. We are Love; that's what we've become. An eternal and unlimited substance. Even the worst attack we can experience has the potential to be the devil defeating himself. "Our righteousness is both a weapon to attack and defend." Forgiveness is a weapon! It teaches us love is a choice, not a feeling. Sometimes people feel they don't love someone any more; but love is a verb. It is something you do or don't do. Choose to love – demonstrate love by empathy, appreciation, affirmation, forgiveness.

Reactive people make love a feeling; they believe what films tell them about love. But the reality is that we are powerful, we control our actions. We choose to love. Leaders are to be proactive people, people who make love a verb. Love is not something you fall into. Love is something you do and give away. Proactive people subordinate feelings to values. They live by faith, not fear. Forgiveness becomes a weapon for good in their hands.

P J Smyth says, *'faith is a fight'*. You don't drift into

faith. You forcibly acquire it. Crossing the line of faith means we live a lifestyle of faith, not fear; hope, not despair; trust, not anxiety. Seeking after eternity, not merely living for the here and now. Leadership and living the adventure depend on a lifestyle of faith. The line we cross is not merely a decision. It is adopting a new way of life, a new attitude. It is making an ongoing, constant faith choice in every circumstance and situation. I can live free from guilt and condemnation through utilising the weapon of forgiveness.

There are so many lies in fear. What stops us living an adventure and a better life? The deception of fear. Have you bought into the lie that you only matter if... (you fill in the blanks). I only matter if I'm smart, successful, strong or whatever. The way manipulative people control others is to attack their identities. When we don't believe, we are good or loveable, we isolate ourselves, hide from vulnerability and intimacy. Intimacy can be seen as In-2-me-u-c. The woman with the issue of blood believed she only mattered if she was healed. Rahab the harlot believed she only mattered if men desired her. When do you matter? Grace is 'Undeservable'. I know strictly there is no such word as 'undeservable' but in the kingdom I think there is!

God is a safe person. A safe person speaks the truth with grace. To experience a meaningful life, we have to be vulnerable, to jump in to change. Fear sees life as a kill or be killed drama. Fear believes all, or at least the majority of people, are out to get me. So there is no trust, and hence no faith or love, and fear rules. God is love, and he gives me the weapon of forgiveness. God did not create love! He **is** love; *agape*, selfless love. Love is the power that created all things – animals, angels, places, planets and people. When I choose love, I choose to live powerful. Fear, anger and frustration no longer become dominant influences in my life. I am powerful by love – God is love (1 John 4:4). Our love for God is a reflection of His love for us. Mark 12:29-31; Love begins and ends with God. But it flows through people (Jn.13:34-5). If God were not personal, He could not be merciful (things do not show mercy). Mercy is the outworking in fallen time and history of the action of a God for whom love of the other is central to His being. God is a giving God. He is a life-giving Father.

God saves His people and shakes evil from the earth. The person who makes a practice of judging others will be judged with the same measure. We are not to live in denial of reality but keep no records of wrongs (1 Corinthians 13:5). Never say "you always, you never you said this before" etc. Whatever you sow, you reap (Galatians 6:7-8). God is judge, not us. He judges equally. God has no favourites! Forgiveness doesn't look for faults in others. Don't allow the small things to upset you – be aware that you may well be upsetting others. Don't be blind to how your attitude, actions and appearance may affect others. Don't meddle in other people's affairs and issues. Stick to your areas of responsibility. Live the adventure.

I am going to face fear whenever I'm on unfamiliar territory – and so is everyone else!

Fear itself is not the problem. It is the authority and power we give it that causes our problems. Fear is an opposite spirit to living from love. Exercise the weapon of forgiveness. Choose to be set apart from the helplessness of fear; live powerfully from love and overcome it. When you know you are loved, you create true 'reality' or truth. It is reckoned (I'm not sure how!) that ninety percent of the things we worry about don't happen. Be positive, not fearful. God is good all the time.

Underlying all our fears is a lack of trust in God and His goodness, a lack of trust in His love and of who we are in Him. Love is seen in the choices we make. *"The last of our human freedoms is the ability to choose our attitude and responses in any and every circumstance"* – Victor Frankl, *Concentration Camp – man's search for meaning.*

Use the weapon of forgiveness – live knowing the old man of sin and its behaviour, thinking, perception and language have been defeated. They are NO LONGER who you are - forgiveness empowers you to let all that go. Instead shift your focus to growing in a perception, thinking and language that are coming from Christ within us.

You are empowered to say "yes" to the new man while simultaneously saying "no" to everything of the old. Don't be of two minds; be of one. As adventurers we may face hard situations – prepare, ask how you should respond in this situation. Your decision-making must flow from a foundation of love and forgiveness.

Forgiveness involves telling the story, naming the hurt and renewing or releasing the relationship. Forgiveness is not forgetting or walking away from accountability or condoning a hurtful act; it's the process of taking back and healing our lives, so we can truly live our adventure.

By the way, to end the story I mentioned earlier. The next day I went into the office to make amends for my error. I went into the car park and looked. What did I see? I saw an old, battered dustbin with my car's red paint on it! No condemnation.

"Courage is not the absence of fear but rather the judgement that something else is more important than fear" – Ambrose Redmoor.

I am limited to three space dimensions. In other words, I can only be in one place at one time. I am limited to one moment at any moment. I cannot travel to the past or future, because in one dimension time is linear. But God is everywhere, all the time. To finite beings time and space seem infinite; but we are on the inside looking out. God is on the outside looking in. Time and space are part of His creation – a day is like a thousand years and a thousand years like a day. A dimension is a way you can move. The number of dimensions determines what is and what is not possible. The more dimensions, the more freedom you have. In a comic, the characters are prisoners of two dimensions. They can move horizontally and vertically. They cannot escape the dimensional surface of the paper. If a comic strip character could take on a third dimension, he could jump right off the page! Utilising the weapon of forgiveness lifts us into a new dimension.

That is also what love does. Love is not just freedom from sin; it's the freedom to use an extra dimension. Faith by prayer enables us to exit our human limitations and dimensions. Powerful loving and living is from a different perspective; a different way of life with different priorities and vision. It is a different kingdom, a different land, a different world (Ephesians 2:10). We are people of resurrection, not death. You and I are a product of our God picture, the internal picture of how we see God. God is love. Powerful people know our problems seem really big when our God is really small. The bigger God is in our perspective, the smaller our challenges are. God wants you to get where God wants you to go more than you want to get where God wants you to go! So He has provided us with the weapon of forgiveness.

Thoughts for your consideration

Have you learned to utilise the power weapon of forgiveness in your own life – in your dealings with yourself and with others?

Do you know you are 'unpunishable'?

Do you know, and does each member of your leadership team, each those you mentor, know God loves you/them?

If so, what does that look like to you and to them in your/their day to day life?

If love and fear are opposites, which is most powerful in your life when major challenges come against you?

What about those in your leadership team and those you mentor? How does this affect those you lead? How can you equip them to live from love?

If love overcomes all things – are you or those you lead or mentor being overcome by things other than love?

If so, what does this look like?

What can you do about it, either for yourself and/or for those you lead or mentor?

How can love empower you and those you lead or mentor to finish well?

What has spoken to you most in this chapter?

CHAPTER 9

Amazing Grace

During a conference on comparative religions, experts from around the world debated what, if any, belief was unique to the Christian faith. They began eliminating possibilities. Incarnation? Other religions had different versions of gods appearing in human form. Resurrection? Again, other religions had accounts of return from death. The debate went on for some time, until C. S. Lewis wandered into the room. "What's the rumpus about?" he asked, and heard in reply that his colleagues were discussing Christianity's unique contribution among world religions. Lewis responded, "Oh that's easy. It's grace." After some discussion, the conferees had to agree. The notion of God's love coming to us free of charge, no strings attached, seems to go against every instinct of humanity. The Buddhist eight-fold path, the Hindu doctrine of karma, the Jewish covenant and the Muslim code of law - each of these offers a way to earn approval. Only Christianity dares to make God's love unconditional.

Law is about rules and regulations. It demands compliance and can become a hard and even harsh taskmaster. In any adventure and within the role of leadership. there is always the temptation to keep to rules and law. They seem clear and safe. Law is also, at least initially, easier for those who are following us to understand and accept. Grace challenges us into relationship, not regulations. Grace inspires us to live for eternity, secure by receiving it. *"Why do we act as though our sin disqualifies us from the grace of God? Grace is the only thing that qualifies us!"* – Mark Batterson, *All In: You Are One Decision Away From a Totally Different Life/*

Grace empowers us to keep following Jesus wherever He leads, because it empowers us to trust. Why? Because the only way we can have a full relationship with God is by Grace (Ephesians 2:8). Grace empowers us to choose life (Deuteronomy 30:19).

Grace provides the power to choose life instead of death, to finish well and not merely seek day-to-day survival.

Grace is essential for enjoying adventure.

Grace is the power of God to transform people and situations

Grace means you need never give up on yourself or on others.

God's grace is sufficient for me. His power is perfected in my weakness (2 Corinthians 12:9)

Grace empowers me to go where in my own strength I feel unable to go.

As I've mentioned, I was born with a cleft palate – I could not speak clearly at all. I was encouraged by my mum, but she also stressed that it would be best not to say much.

In 1981, when I was baptised, I received from God in His grace – *"Open your mouth and I will fill it."* "No," I said, "I can't! No one will understand me – it is impossible." God said, "Trust me and see what I will do – my power is perfected in your weakness". Many years later, I can testify to having been involved in founding and then leading a church for thirty years; to having seen many lives transformed for eternity; to having preached and ministered in Africa, America, Europe and Asia – Four continents! How? God's amazing grace! His power is perfected in my weakness. His grace is sufficient for me to live an adventure. Grace is the key to life. It is amazing grace that empowers us to live fully for God, and that saves us from eternal death. Grace is not 'fair'. We do not 'deserve it'. Grace is unmerited, unending, unfailing, unlimited. Grace empowers us, and we need to live it with others. As God's child, you have access to a priceless gift: grace. While God wants you to do your best in every situation, you never have to worry that it won't be enough. God's grace will meet you wherever you are. It will help you accomplish everything He wants you to do in life. When you rely on His amazing grace rather than just your own limited power, you'll discover His abundant life. Grace is the fuel for your adventure!

As Christians we are ambassadors from another world, modelling a different kingdom, a different lifestyle. No one can do everything, but for me my adventure is to seek to address underlying structures and foundational issues to bring about change.

Grace is a culture. Culture is the world in which we are born and the world that is born in us. Put another way, the world in which we live and the world that lives in us. Culture is the comprehensive, penetrating context that encompasses our life, thought, art, speech, entertainment, responsibilities, values and faith. The essence of culture in regard to its most profound challenge is that it is a spirit; a perspective on the world. It doesn't simply give a context for our values, it shapes our values, because it has values in and of itself. It doesn't just provide the atmosphere for something such as communication; it forms what communication is and how it is achieved. Culture alters not only what is said but what is heard – and how. Grace enables me to live positively towards myself and others.

Even when we live by grace, conflict can arise. When conflict arises, ask what is the most generous assumption you can make about this person, what they have said or done? Robert Bolton identifies three kinds of conflict:

- Conflict of emotions.
- Values conflict.
- Conflict of needs.

Whatever the cause of the conflict, listening and grace are essential. It is not enough to hear; hearing does not resolve conflict. We need to listen with grace. The goal of any confrontation is to restore connection. Grace empowers reconnection.

Grace seeks to understand, and only then to be understood. Grace is generous. Grace believes the other person is doing the best they can in their current situation. Grace never judges, condemns or writes off self or others. Grace is power, not weakness. Living by grace is living powerful. Grace empowers you to forgive instead of being a victim consumed by anger and hatred. Fear and desperation can result in violence. Grace overcomes resentment Nelson Mandela said: *"Resentment is like drinking poison and expecting it to kill your enemies"*. Grace empowers you to connect with others, to receive with an open heart and give with an open heart. Grace empowers you to be compassionate – a relationship of equals, suffering with the other. Grace empowers you to be courageous – to be performing acts of courage, and sharing your vulnerability with others. Grace empowers us to change to succeed in our adventure. In our story or adventure, grace is Act 3; it is the end of the story. In the story of your life, Act 1 has already happened, Act 2 is happening and Act 3 will happen. What outcome in integrity do you desire?

Grace anticipates growth and positive change and sees and works towards them.

A professor put a blank piece of paper with a black dot on an exam question, face down. When the students turned over the paper they were asked to respond to what they saw. All of the students described and focused on the black dot.

Later the Professor told his students that life would

have its problems and difficulties, like the black dot. Then he said, "But if you focus on that rather than all the white space or blessings around it, you will become negative, fearful and anxious." Grace empowers us to focus on blessings, not the black dots.

Grace is the key to life. It is grace that saves us from eternal death (Ephesians 2:8). When God breaks through in power grace, we must follow through in process.

It happened one lovely day in America. My wife and I were celebrating our silver wedding with our two young sons and staying with friends in Missouri. Our friends took us to a place called 'Johnson Shut-ins.' It was a series of what looked like pools surrounded by grass or rocks down to the river. Caleb, our youngest son did not want to go as it was quite a long way down to the bottom where the river was, so he stayed with our American friends at the top. Linda and I and Pete went to explore.

As we went in, I noticed a man at the side. There was something about him that drew my eyes to him (not what normally happens to me with men)! As we progressed, I was more timid, not being able to swim particularly well. Pete wanted to go faster, so Linda went off with him. I said I would follow them down at my own pace. It was certainly a beautiful spot, with lots of people sunbathing around the sides of the pools.

As we went further down, there were fewer people about and the pools started to get deeper and deeper. Initially I had been able to wade across quite easily, but this was getting harder and harder.

I came down to another pool. This time I realised I would need to swim across. That was fine. I came down to another pool, so I thought I would do it again. I launched myself off from the side when suddenly a boy jumped off the rocks and landed right in front of me. I had to stop swimming. I began to sink and feel myself drowning. I tried not to panic, but suddenly as I put my hand up someone grabbed it. They pulled me with one strong pull straight up out of the water and on to the bank a few feet above. I spluttered, looked around and saw the man who I had noticed at the start of this adventure. As I said "thank you", he disappeared, and I never saw him again.

As I contemplated the whole event afterwards I realised how much strength the man must have had to pull me straight up out of the water and on to the bank. I believe he was an angel. The Bible says angels are sent to minister help to the heirs of salvation. This man, or angel, certainly rescued me!

Recently I reviewed the Johnson Shut-ins website; it says "Splash off in nature's waterpark – the shut-ins. Swimming is at your own risk." (Now they tell me!) But then again, if I hadn't tried to swim I might not have seen the angel nor have experienced God's grace this way.

Thoughts for your consideration

What does grace mean for you?

How would you differentiate between grace and law?

Have you experienced grace in your life? When? What did it look like?

Have you demonstrated grace to others? How?

Why does it always seem easier to live by law than grace?

For you or your team/mentees

Does grace mean that you can do whatever you like and it doesn't matter, as it is covered by God's grace? Why? If not, what does it mean? For you/your team/those you mentor?

If you are saved by Grace, does that mean Grace is powerful? If Grace is powerful enough to save you from all the powers of hell in order to bring you to Christ, then do you consider Grace is powerful enough for you to live by day by day? How can you equip those in your team, those you mentor and those you lead to experience daily the power of grace?

What has spoken to you most in this chapter?

CHAPTER 10

Growth mindset

With a fixed mindset, you believe that you are who you are, and you cannot change. This creates problems when you're challenged, because anything that appears to be more than you can handle is bound to make you feel hopeless and overwhelmed. Success in life is how you deal with failure. Does failure define that you are a failure? Or does failure give you information from which to try something different to grow from? People with a growth mindset believe that they can improve, with effort.

How we think determines how we act. The Bible says that how a man thinks in his heart, so he is, or so he lives. Growth is a mindset before it becomes an action. Growth relates to consequences and responsibility, not punishment. Growth calls forth growth from ourselves and others, not out of pressure but out of love. Our adventure involves calling ourselves and others into all we can be in God.

A person with a fixed mindset reveals this in their conversations with themselves and others. They say or hear words like 'I can't change', 'it's too hard', I don't want to', I'm happy as I am', 'it's alright for them or you' and such like. Growth requires us to adopt a different mindset, a mindset which doesn't focus on our failures or disappointments. To live the adventure involves shooting down all areas of fear that show their head above the parapet. *"Failure isn't fatal, but failure to change might be"* – John Wooden.

Growth is here to stay. Don't settle for the lifestyle adopted by some that says "once saved, always saved". You've said the prayer, you're saved, that's enough. I exhort you to keep growing and living your adventure. I'm not arguing whether "once saved always saved" is true or not. What I am saying is don't settle, keep growing, there is always more to learn and receive in God. Adopt a mindset of seeking and continually desiring to grow.

The church is full of people who have been touched but not changed. A settling mentality, not a growth mentality. It is a work of the Spirit to empower us to be born again. However, a key component to living this out day by day lies in the mind. Transformation comes through the renewing of the mind (Romans 12:2). Give your mind a job to do, or else it will find a job to do on its own! Think constructively and positively about life change and growth. Otherwise your mind will focus itself on the negative and the destructive.

Walking in the light increases our capacity to exceed the darkness around us and the negativity that it brings. It allows us the opportunity to learn how to overcome; to prevail in all circumstances and succeed in our adventure. Consider your current situation and any darkness that still clings to you, where anxiety, fear and doubt may have penetrated to you. Then consider the light that may have entered your life, the insight provided by prophecy or by personal revelation. Learn to walk and grow within this light, step by step. Whether it's a lamp to your feet or a light to your path, live in the Light of the Lord – out of the darkness into the day. I always feel so desperate when people say their loved ones were saved but are no longer walking with God. Be an inspiration and a Godly provocation by your love. *"You are God's love gift to others"*, especially your family.

Life is about growing. When you were young your nappies were changed for you, but as you grow, you didn't need that. When you were young, you were spoon fed; as you grow you learn to feed yourself. Spiritually too, learn and seek to grow yourself and live the adventure. Turn challenges and failures into opportunities to overcome, and don't play the blame and shame game. A growth mindset is a buffer against defeatism. It reframes failure as a natural part of the change process.

People only persevere if they see falling down as learning rather than failing – you can see this in the life of any toddler! Any form of growth involves change.

For me in my adventure, a specific opportunity for growth happened when I was working as a management accountant with Christies' of London. Christies' had only a year or two earlier taken over a stamp auctioneers I was working for in Bournemouth and they continued to employ me. I thoroughly enjoyed management accountancy. I found it challenging and rewarding, particularly financially. We had moved into what I considered to be my dream house in the small Dorset town of Wimborne. It was a dream because not only was it well positioned, I was able to walk all around it in my own garden. Funny things, dreams! Anyway, whilst I was thoroughly enjoying my job, my life, my pregnant wife and young son, I began to realise that there was something deeper missing from my life. My job was great, but it wasn't fully giving me purpose and destiny. What was the adventure for me?

As a follower of Jesus Christ, I sought Him. I quickly began to realise He wanted me to lead a church. Wow! But God. From my mind came all the reasons why it could not be me. Family, comfort, success and most of all I had a cleft palate. How could I ever lead a church? How could I afford to lead a church? No church could afford to pay my current salary, and I needed that to meet my mortgage payments on my dream house. You may or may not have experienced it, but God does speak to us today. God revealed to me a scripture that I had not noticed before; it said *"the borrower becomes the lender's slave"*. And then I felt a quiet voice deep on the inside of me ask: *"whose slave are you?"* (Proverbs 22:7).

I realised that I would have to be willing to sell my 'dream' house and move down market. Perhaps I could buy a house without a mortgage? This would be amazing, I thought, because my DIY skills are non-existent. Both Linda and I struggled and struggled with this change, for different reasons. Eventually we submitted to God and accepted what we believed was His will for us, a new adventure. After a while we found a house which we could afford without a mortgage in Parkstone, Dorset, and moved in with our two sons. At around the same time the church was launched, a new adventure began, and the rest, as they say, is history.

Story is important to developing a growth mindset and living an adventure beyond our own experience, knowledge and limitations. What do you feel about the story you are telling yourself? Does it make you happy, fulfilled, sad, frustrated, excited, passive or passionate? Why? What is the root of the story you are telling yourself? Where does it come from? We are wired for story, and in the absence of 'data' we will rely on our own story about a situation or conspiracy. What we speak impacts our mentality towards growth. *"Never say never, because limits like fears are often just an illusion"* – Michael Jackson. *"If you are trying to achieve there will be obstacles, but they don't have to stop you. If you run into a wall, don't turn around and give up. Figure how to climb it go through it or work around it"* – Michael Jordan. Everything is hard before it is easy – remember learning to drive a car.

What looks like a person problem is often a situation problem. We often attribute people's behaviour to the way they are, rather than to the situation they are in, or feel they are in.

People are incredibly sensitive to their environment and culture. They want to fit in; behaviour is contagious! This is true for the Gospel. We need to make it feel "cool", meaningful, normal, sensible, exciting and wise. It is!

Picasso was a terrible colourist. Turner could not paint human beings. Saul Steinberg's formal drafting skills were appalling. T.S. Eliot had a full-time day job. Henry Miller was a wildly uneven writer. Bob Dylan can't sing or play guitar. But that did not stop them, right? So I guess the next question is "Why not?" Why should it? They choose to live their adventure with a growth mentality. People with a growth mentality find their voice and inspire others to find theirs. Voice is unique personal significance. Voice lies at the nexus of talent (your natural gifts and strengths), passion (those things that naturally energise, excite, motivate or inspire you), need (including what the world needs enough to pay for), conscience (that still small voice within you that assures you what is right and prompts you to do it) and Spirit (being led by the Holy Spirit and empowered by Him to do God's will and purpose).

Change starts when we look in a mirror and become self-aware. We notice that there is some blemish or change that needs to be addressed. Self-awareness begins the process of either a growth mentality or a fixed mindset. When we overcome our fear of losing something, we find our view of the future more peace-filled and less self-centred. When this change first occurs in you, it will radiate out from you to other people. They will see your adventure producing growth. They will watch your bold, brave, powerful example of self-awareness turning to positive action in your own life. When that happens you have just planted a seed of change, growth and adventure into others, unconsciously giving others a powerful roadmap to change the direction of their lives, to embrace growth and adventure.

Half of growth is learning what we don't know. The other half is unlearning what we do know! It often feels easier and more comfortable to lead out of what you know and have experienced before. It worked before, why change it? Would you say you have a growth mentality? How is it demonstrated? How do you speak? *"Don't judge those who try and fail; only those who fail to try."*

Successes make you clever, but failures make you wise. Albert Einstein defined insanity as *"doing the same thing over and over and expecting a different result."* Growth involves change; start with and focus on changing yourself. Remember, big changes come from a succession of small changes. It's OK if the first changes seem trivial; you are on an adventure of growth. Movement produces its own momentum.

Authority is the right to 'author'. God has exclusive rights to write the script for our lives. However, we also have a responsibility to script our own story, in line with God's plan. Powerful people tell or write their story in line with His Story. Powerful people understand *"Growth never just happens. You have to be intentional about it."* We won't live forever on this earth, so powerful people desire to pour into the Red Sea, not the Dead Sea.

Your life is a gift from God to you. It has infinite value to Him, which He communicates to you. Peter Scazzero writes: *"What we seek is long term inner transformation into the image of Christ for the sake of the world"*. Albert Einstein once said: *"Significant problems that we face cannot be solved at the same level of thinking we were at when we created them."* You must learn to think in a new way – you need a "paradigm shift."

Michael Jordan, the star basketball player, said *"You miss 100% of the shots you don't take"*.

On a personal level I've noticed that when people are "stuck" in life, it is because they are usually continuing to frame their problem with a set of assumptions that no longer apply. They use the same problem-solving techniques they used in the past, even though they don't work any more. In other words, they are acting from a fixed mindset. The fixed or powerless mindset adopts a blame/shame culture. When something goes wrong, it is never their fault always someone else's. John McEnroe: "You cannot be serious!" It is the linesman's fault, the referee's fault or even the crowd's fault!

Growth is stopped by a fixed mindset. The person with a fixed mindset looks through negative lenses (like wearing dark sunglasses in a dark room). They say it's hopeless, it will never change – they stop living an adventure. Life looks dark, hard and unsafe.

In any or every area of life - marriage, relationships, work – we can become single-sighted or adopt a fixed mindset. This leaves us vulnerable. We become easily hurt and withdraw to protect ourselves. We shut down from new ideas instead of embracing our adventure. We are existing, not living an adventure. Instead of passion, passivity rules; we become apathetic and lukewarm and adopt a coping mentality.

Growth has to overcome a fear of taking risks. A fixed mindset settles for security and safety. Out of anxiety and concern about what 'could happen', it develops a critical, cynical and pessimistic attitude. Instead of determination, stubbornness arises. Fixed mindset people seek to control in order to overcome their fear – but it will only get even worse! A fixed mindset, instead of seeking to change, merely dreams. People dream about the results they desire from life and wonder why they remain just that – dreams. Dreams without goals will always remain dreams. So we need to make changes that count.

Consider the following six questions carefully. Each addresses a critical area of life that may need improvement.

What areas of my thinking do I need to change?

What beliefs do I hold that hold me back?

What expectations hinder my personal growth?

What attitudes hurt my success?

What behavioural areas must I change to give me a boost?

What things are keeping me from a peak performance?

Developing a growth mindset requires creating a clear, compelling vision of how things can be different. Change rarely occurs when vision is lacking, blurry or too complicated.

Keep the vision before yourself and others. When the vision fades, momentum dies.

Identify and get rid of the obstacles that prevent change.

Plan for short term wins on the way to ultimate long-term lasting change. Celebrate intermediate positive changes when they come.

Don't stop the process, or declare victory too soon. Premature victory celebrations kill momentum. And then the powerful forces associated with tradition take over.

Reinforce the changes. This involves emphasising that "this new way is how we do things now.

When you change your thinking, you change your beliefs.

When you change your beliefs, you change your expectations.

When you change your expectations, you change your attitude.

When you change your attitude, you change your behaviour.

When you change your behaviour, you change your performance.

When you change your performance, you change your life.

Choose to adopt a growth mindset. Life involves growing. Every living thing grows. Growth is about developing, moving forward, pressing on to the upward call of God in Christ Jesus (Phil. 3:14). It is vital to live an adventure so that we do not become passive, apathetic and faithless. When we conform to the world, we are tempted to accept a fixed mindset.

Fixed mindsets relies on our experience, but so often anxiety and fear of failure kick in. The world offers self-worth through effort, hard work, competition or comparison. However this mindset is dependent on results - or what others think of our results! We become like ostriches and bury our heads.

Instead of growth, we develop a bystander mentality – Watch, wait and do nothing. Growth is a mindset and acceptance of change – it actively makes a choice not to live from a fixed mindset!

Thoughts for your consideration

Have you or each person in your team/mentees a growth mindset or a fixed mindset? How do you/they know?

What does a growth mindset look like for you, and for each of your team members/mentees?

Powerful/powerless questions to consider – for you and for each of your team

> Do you like the direction you are headed?
>
> If you keep going down this road, where will you end up?
>
> What will people say about you when you die?
>
> What is one thing you can change about your life today to make the ending of your story better? What about those in your leadership team/mentees?

What has spoken to you most in this chapter?

CHAPTER 11

Trust and betrayal

On any adventure, trust is important. We need to be able to trust ourselves, our companions and our situation. Trust is founded on identity - for instance, knowing who you are – and *whose* you are! As well as knowing the hearts of those around you. Trust enables you to be secure in the midst of the mystery of the Kingdom, now and not yet! I can lead and pray in trust, whether or not I see the outcomes I desire. Trust relates to faith, and can often be transposed. Trust doesn't mean blind trust regardless; rather trust is about believing that growth, change and development can occur in the person you trust.

Trust involves delegation. Delegation is not allowing others to make the decision as long as it is done your way. That is not delegation – it is bad leadership. As Walter C. Wright says in *Relational Leadership*: *"Delegation develops ownership and responsibility in others. Delegation is the process of moving the decision point from the leader to the follower."*

Being on an adventure, being a leader, or even just a human being, makes trust so vital, yet so hard. I know in my adventure and leadership people who have, at least from my perspective, let me down. I remember walking through a church split and receiving many negative handwritten letters. I almost developed a fear of receiving these. They were extremely antagonistic and hurtful – how could I trust again? I had poured my life into many of these folks. Suddenly, for reasons that probably neither I nor they fully grasped, they were angry and negative towards me. I remember a situation where a particular person in the midst of all of the difficulties said to me, "Dave, I know that lots of people are being hurtful to you right now, but I want you to know I am with you and for you I will not leave you." A week later, he handed in his resignation!

As a person on an adventure and as a leader, it is important that trust is first and foremost in God. It is written in John's Gospel that *"Jesus never entrusted himself to any man, for he knew what was in their hearts."* This means Jesus, and it's the same for us, trusted people, trusted what they said, but didn't build His life, adventure or ministry on them. We serve God. It is only through God that we can effectively serve people. It is because we trust God that we have a powerful trust, a trust which is not dependent on what others do to you. Our focus is to be eternal; not merely the immediate.

Was Judas a risk for Jesus? This point was driven home to me a few years ago. I experienced being betrayed by one of my best friends. I was really hurting and feeling disillusioned. I began to express from my heart: *"I will never trust anyone like that again. I am going to put safeguards and double-checks into our church structure that require a high degree of accountability. I will never let someone do this to me again."*

Yet the Bible says Judas was a thief and Jesus knew it (John 12:4-7). Jesus made Judas the treasurer of His ministry. Why would Jesus make Judas the treasurer when He knew that he was a thief?" There are only two reasons I can think of. First is that Jesus was trying to make Judas fail. That doesn't seem like the Jesus I know. The second reason is that Jesus developed a culture of faith around Himself. This faith culture was manifested in Jesus allowing people to either live up to His faith in them or to live down to their faith in themselves. This culture of trust/faith eventually resulted in eleven men becoming world-changers and one man hanging himself. World-changers are only developed in a culture of faith. Faith requires risk, and the nature of risk is that sometimes you lose.

It is good to be wise and require accountability, but if you stop believing in your people you won't create world-changers. While I believe in people around me, it is the people who have believed in me who have actually changed me the most. If you don't produce a Judas now and then, you don't trust people as much as you should and you are reducing the number of Peters you will produce. The Kingdom is entered into by faith, lived in through faith, and extended with faith manifested through risk. This is what trust looks like from a Kingdom of God perspective. There's a reason why the One sent to guide you into the realms of the Spirit is called the Comforter. If you follow Him, you're going to need one! So today I want to encourage you on your adventure to actively take a risk, to step outside your comfort zone.

Without a sure and certain trust in God we will be

unable to empower others to trust during their times of difficulty. I remember one dear lady had experienced some miscarriages. She continued to trust God. Eventually she gave birth to two wonderful children. Trust takes us beyond our own circumstances and calls us towards God. Trust can lead to joy. I have experienced the pain of loved ones dying of suffering, great pain or distress or losing jobs, money, homes. I have learnt to cry well. When I don't have the answer, I just have to cry, or as Jesus Himself put it, "weep with those that weep". Happiness is tied to circumstances. Joyfulness is tied to trusting God.

Trust enables us to press into and experience the joy of breakthrough, of healing, of transformation, and of seeing people saved for eternity. Laugh well when these things happen. Even the angels rejoice over one sinner who repents. Laughter is good medicine; the Psalmist says it does good to our souls (mind – thinking, and will – choices and emotions – feelings).

The Greek word for Happiness is *makarios,* and it is tied to things or events. The Greek word for Joy is *chario* and it is tied to our being. It is said that the opposite of joy is not sadness but fear, ie a lack of trust. When we are ruled by scarcity, we think not experiencing joy will cause any loss to hurt less, so we live from a negative hope. However Joy is rooted in being, knowing that there is enough and we are enough. Joy is what happens when we allow ourselves to recognise how good things really are.

Joy is who God is, where He lives from and what He does. God lives in perpetual, everlasting and eternal joy. In His Presence there is fullness of joy. The Father does not give us joy; He gives us Himself. He is absolute joy personified. The atmosphere surrounding God is always joyful. We need to anchor our souls in the person of God and embrace His uninhibited delight in all things.

When we rejoice, it is because we have entered the place of His joy and delight. It means we are trusting God, whatever, wherever, whenever. We centre ourselves in His joy. We breathe it in. We smile because we live under His smile. We rejoice because He is delight, and delightful, and delights in us as we respond to Him in faith (Hebrews 11:6).

Whenever we encounter God's Kingdom, we are lovingly confronted with the God who loves to celebrate. We come under the influence of His innate joyfulness. When life is tough, then we have permission to count it all joy (James 1:23). Joy is meant to overwhelm every negative emotion. "Sorrow and sighing may last for a night, but joy comes in the morning" (Psalm 30:5), ie the presence of God. When joy is present, no negative emotion can flourish. Jesus was acquainted with grief (Isaiah 53:3); it was not a close traveling companion. We need to be restored to the joy of our salvation, the delight and pleasure of our first major contact with the Lord. My Joy keeps all experience in God fresh. New every morning is God's goodness and compassion (Lamentations 3:21–23). Life in the Spirit is renewable daily, and joy is always a part of God's day for us. It is His plan for us to be joyful on a constant basis. "These things I have spoken to you that your joy may be full!" (John 15:11).

There is, or was, an employee policy at Legoland that says that employees should "present" (open-palm gesture) their directions instead of "pointing" them. This is because the open-palmed gesture conveys trust, making people more likely to agree with what you're saying and find you friendly and likeable. Pointing, on the flip side, is generally seen as aggressive and rude.

For many, the ability to trust people is shaped in infancy. From the moment we enter the world, our deepest need is to love and be loved by other human beings, to develop lasting relational bonds. This need is met as we consistently complete trust cycles in our interactions with other people, specifically with our primary caregivers.

A trust cycle is completed when:
You have a need
The need is expressed
There is a response to the need
The need is satisfied

Here is the problem: this trust cycle can break down at any point. Trust is damaged if people fail to identify and express, lovingly, openly and honestly, their needs. Trust can be damaged if the other person does not respond to that expressed need, or responds in a negative way.

Unfortunately we will all probably experience broken trust in life. Most of us experience it in childhood, simply because all parents, even the best of them, are human beings who make mistakes. Parents bring their own areas of brokenness into parenting. If wounds are not healed and truth and trust restored, they will fester, damaging our ability to create intimacy and connection in relationships. We all approach relationships with a basic question: "Can I trust you? Can I trust you with my heart? Can I trust you to love me unconditionally and help meet the need for relationship in my life?"

To live a fulfilled adventure, our overall trust must be in God and not in human beings. When look at people through a powerless lens of wounding and mistrust, we try to answer the question 'can I trust you?' based on our best guess. We try and guess what the other person is going to do or how they will respond to us. When we make the change into powerful thinking, we recognise that trust is a choice, a choice we can make independently of what the other person does. Just as Jesus chose to trust Judas, even though He knew Judas would betray Him, so we make the powerful choice to say "I will trust you. You don't control my trust. I do." I choose to have faith that you can change, but it is your responsibility and choice whether or not you live up to my faith in you.

As leaders and adventurers, we are to empower people to break a pattern of mistrust, of powerlessness and dysfunctional relationships. We must confirm to ourselves and others these core messages as truth:

1. We were made to love and be loved.

    Often during our adventure, life impacts us negatively. We experience unmet needs. Then broken trust attacks our sense of value and worthiness. The truth is God created us to love and be loved.

2. I can express my deep needs.

    All of us have needs. The need to be comforted, encouraged, championed and loved unconditionally. We need to learn to express these needs in healthy ways. Start with simple 'I' messages with the people closest to you. For example: "I am feeling discouraged right now. I need to be encouraged and reminded of who I really am." At times this can feel scary and vulnerable, but it is a key path into trust.

3. I can trust, believe in and be intimate with others. Our most satisfying experience as human beings is to be completely known and accepted for who we are. We can experience this in safe intimate relationships built on trust. Intimacy – *"into-me-you-see."*

We have to learn how to express and meet one another's needs. Then we can say "We can fully be ourselves together, because you can see into me and I can see into you.

When you wonder if you can trust someone, challenge yourself to give a powerful answer: "I can trust you because I choose to trust you." Trust must flow from our trust in God. Only out of this trust can we consciously give trust to another. Being confident in God's trustworthiness empowers me to add value to you. Goethe expounded the fruit of trust when he wrote: *"Treat a man as he is and he will remain as he is; treat a man as he can and should be and he will become as he can and should be"*. Trust is a verb. You can entrust someone and give them responsibility. Trust results from knowledge. We either live from natural knowledge or knowledge of God. You can trust someone because of who they have proven to be, or you can trust because of who God has proven to be.

Trust and faith are from the same root word in Greek. Faith involves a loss of control. In life there is always an element of uncertainty. God is always calling us into *terra incognita* - an unknown or unexplored area – God says 'Behold, I do something new!' He wants us to go where we've never been before and do what we've never done. It is only by trust and faith that powerful people dare to take the risk, confident that God is good.

The servant who buries his talent is called wicked. Why? Because he isn't willing to live by faith (take a calculated risk – trust). How we explain events to ourselves determines how much we are living by faith and trust. James Gleick says "*tiny differences in input can quickly become overwhelming differences in output*" (the 'butterfly effect').

When we learn and study scripture we literally 'upgrade' our minds. In effect, we are 'downloading' the mind of Christ. (Rm.12:2) Jesus said... you have heard it said... But I say to you... We stop thinking human thoughts and start thinking God thoughts, ie we trust and have faith in who He is. To live by trust often means unlearning. Unlearning involves overcoming irrational fears and misconceptions that keep us from operating as we were designed to do (in faith/trust – Genesis 3; Hebrews 1:1).

Trust involves trusting yourself. Unless you trust

yourself, you will never be able to fully have faith in and trust others.

I consider that the world's insistence on confidentiality is a trap. People either trust you or they don't. In the words of Jesus, let your yes be yes and your no be no. Don't swear you will never tell anyone else. Don't allow yourself to be imprisoned by confidentiality. If you live a life of trust, people will either trust you or not; that is their choice and call.

People have come to me and said "can I tell you something in confidence?" I have always replied "I have no secrets from my wife and no secrets from my fellow elders." If that means they can't tell me, then that's fine. They will either trust me or not. I need to be free to talk if I'm told something that needs a direct intervention or needs more wisdom than I have, or is weighing heavy on me and I need to unburden myself. Now this doesn't mean that I will tell my wife or my fellow elders, but it does mean I am free to if I decide I need to. I have known many people really suffer from being bound by the prison of confidentiality. My advice is, don't let it happen to you.

Trusting others doesn't mean they won't make mistakes. It means that if they, or you, make a mistake, you will act together to rectify it. Be powerful – be patient, authentic and consistent and trust will come. Discipleship purposely cultivates deep connections and provides a place to share fears and challenges and develop a sense of trust in your adventure.

Did you hear about the inventor of the MRI scanner? He was delighted with his invention as it helped people. Then he saw children being terrified of having to go through this tube. He wanted to change their perception. He wanted to replace their fear with faith and trust. He decided to paint the room like a treasure island and the tube like a pirate ship. He then told the children that to find the treasure they would have to go through the tube. They would have to be very still, because otherwise the pirates would know they were there! At the end they found some treasure. He knew he had succeeded when one little girl said to her mummy on the way out, "Mummy, can we come back again tomorrow?"

Thoughts for your consideration

Has your trust ever been broken or betrayed? How do you feel about it? How do you live after that experience? What about your team members/mentees?

Are you able to express your genuine needs to your spouse and to your fellow leaders and those you mentor? Are they also in turn able to express their needs to you? Do they? Are they?

How do others respond when you express your needs?

Are others able to express their true needs to you?

Are you able to express gratitude? When?

What has spoken to you most in this chapter?

CHAPTER 12
Good foundations

Living my adventure required me to understand about being an ambassador from another world, modelling a different kingdom and lifestyle. In God's kingdom we are to address underlying structures and foundational issues in the world and the church to bring about change as appropriate

Jesus spent over ninety percent of his life – thirty out of thirty-three years – in obscurity. In those hidden years he built a strong and lifelong foundation of relationship with the Father. If it was necessary for

Jesus, how much more important for you and me. Yet I know I often found it easier to skimp on investing in my time with God. When I did, I always suffered the consequences. Living powerful lives requires the foundation of time and an intimate relationship with the Father. Foundations are the essential element to any building and adventure, and to any form of leadership which seeks to build something to last. Build on good foundations.

Jesus told a story of foundations: *"Everyone therefore who hears these words of mine and does them I will liken him to a wise man who built his house on a rock. The rain came down the floods came and the winds blew and beat on that house; and it didn't fall for it was founded on the rock."* (Matthew 7:24-7). Even from an early age we are taught the importance of good foundations. There is a children's story about three pigs and a big bad wolf. The first pig built a house of straw; the wolf blew it down. The second pig built a house of wood and the wolf blow that one down too. The first two pigs wanted to play instead of building a house that would last. The third pig laid strong foundations and built a house of brick. That house was able to stand.

Foundations are what we build on. A building is only as strong as its foundations. A tree is only as strong as its roots. Foundations in our lives must be secure and firm to enable a building or plant to flourish and grow. Our foundations are to last for eternity and beyond. They must hold us secure, whatever storms we face in this life. I have written a separate course outlining some basic theological foundations. However, the greatest foundation has to be intimacy - fully knowing and being fully known by God.

"We can easily forgive a child who is afraid of the dark; the real tragedy of life is when men are afraid of the light" – Plato.

Truth is truth, but unless it becomes your truth it will not change your life; what you do matters, everything else is just talk. Jesus said, *"I am the way the truth and the life"* (John 14:6). The Psalmist writes *"If the foundations are destroyed, what can the righteous do?"* Psalm11:3 also See foundations re Isaiah 28:14-28; Luke 6:46ff.

God Himself must be our ultimate foundation. He is our source, our creator, our redeemer. God's love, character, word and Spirit are key foundations for our lives. Laying good foundations requires us to wrestle with the question "in what way does my current pace of life and leadership enhance or diminish my ability to allow God's will and presence full access to my life?" God's will must be our foundation, not 'busyness'. Our foundation must be that success is founded not on circumstances or outcomes but in knowing God intimately and personally.

My prophetic calling is to lay, test and examine foundations in individuals, families, churches and communities (Jeremiah 1:5-10; Isaiah 62:10). Godly foundations of word, Spirit and relationship with God equip and empower disciples to see everyman complete in Christ (Colossians 1:28; Isaiah 61:1-4). Peter Scazzero, in his wonderful book *The Emotionally Healthy Leader*, constantly identifies the importance of good foundations. We need to make time for Jesus to 'know us' (Matthew 7:21-23). Good foundations require us to not merely know about God and His word. We are to take time to be known by Him in every area of our life and leadership.

When a child (or adult) is having a tantrum, he is saying "notice me, understand me, meet my need". However tantrums indicate that they are feeling insecure - their foundations suddenly feel shaky. Like everyone else they desire love, security, acceptance and acknowledgement.

Foundations are essential if our future is to grow strong and healthy. The French resistance fighter Stéphane Hessel urged the rising generation of social justice activists to remember the fight he and others had put up during the drafting of the 1948 Universal Declaration of Human Rights. The foundation for them was the word 'universal', not 'international', as proposed by the main governments. They did this knowing that arguments about sovereignty would sooner or later be advanced to deny rights. The tragedy today is that there is not a single democratic government on Earth prepared to defend that principle. They will issue notes of displeasure over some deaths or crackdowns, but they refuse to restate the universality of the principles these actions violate. The foundation of universal principles has to begin with individual people. Living from foundations ensures we keep restating to ourselves and those around us that our human rights are, as the 1948 declaration states, "equal and inalienable". Thus if one faraway kleptocrat steals them from his subjects, that is like stealing them from ourselves. The foundations we lay are the essential ingredient in the success or otherwise of any building. The foundation of life, the way we live and how we interact are essential if we are to build successfully and effectively for the good of God's world.

In many cases this world lays its foundations based on culture. However, culture is a floating and unstable foundation. What is culture? The Latin word means we do not just leave nature as it is but make something of it, eg cultivate it, as in agriculture, horticulture etc. In other words, culture by its very nature is fluid and changeable. In the twenty-first century, the world tries to create a culture of easy sex; pornography, even computer games like Grand Theft Auto encourage you to be a criminal, murderer or even a rapist. There is a culture of gender confusion whereby nobody can challenge anyone else's lifestyle. This arises because there is no agreed foundation or fixed compass point to refer back to.

Godly foundations provide inspiration for transformation from the inside out. There is a story by Hans Christian Andersen which illustrates the flimsiness of culture. Apparently there once was an Emperor who loved new clothes and wanted the latest fashions. One day two swindlers came into town knowing the king's weakness for showing off the latest fashions, and they persuaded him to buy a new suit. However the suit did not exist. They persuaded the Emperor that only wise and clever people could see it. So the Emperor passed the story around his court. Everyone wanted to be thought of as wise, so when the Emperor came out of his rooms wearing the new suit, ie nothing, everyone was full of praise. However, when the Emperor left the palace, a servant boy saw him. The boy yelled out that the king was naked. The deception was exposed, but the swindlers had escaped long before with their ill-gotten gains.

In this world, culture depends on opinion and not

God's foundation. In today's world, truth is no longer accepted as foundational. Rather truth is regarded as personal and isolated. What's true for you may not be true for me. Having strong foundations empowers us to resist evil and stand for what is good (James 4:7; Phil. 4:8). Be holy as He is holy, eg seek to create a foundation of holiness; ie live and have vision and values according to God's word, whatever the world does or says (Matthew 6:33).

God HIMSELF is to be our foundation. There is one transcendent, sovereign all-powerful God who created all things. God is good – nothing or no-one else is! The way we live comes from who we worship. We either worship good/perfect – God - or what is not perfect. Then our worship corrupts and pollutes, and this negatively affects the foundations of the life we live.

On a visit to Carthage I found the Tunisians had uncovered the remains of a Roman civilisation under the place where they now lived. Underneath that was a foundation of the Carthaginian civilisation. Likewise, in previous generations we had foundations laid in our lives, physical, emotional and spiritual. In the womb, foundations were laid. In our early preschool years, new foundations were laid. On top of that, there was early childhood; puberty, teenage years and adulthood foundations, all laid on top of one civilisation or way of life. However beneath them all lies the foundation of Christ. This was laid before the foundation of the world! This foundation reveals our true identity, purpose and destiny on Planet Earth. Herein lies true security; self-worth, significance and adventure.

It is vital we lay good foundations. Matthew 13:11 says we have been given to know the mysteries of the Kingdom. We are to use this revelation to unlock eternal destinies and impossible situations or circumstances. Prophecy in part is calling into being things that were not (Romans 4:17). Prophecy does not merely predict the future, it helps to create it. People on an adventure ask, are these foundations from the world the past, my experiences, the culture or from God? 1 Corinthians 14:3 tells us that one of the purposes of prophecy is edification; the Greek word is *oikodome*. Oikodome refers to the act of building a home and a life - hence stressing the importance of good foundations. We lay Godly foundations by grace hope and faith. When God gives a child to parents (physical and/or spiritual), that child comes prepackaged with a set of GIFTS and callings. Each person is uniquely his or her own. Inside every child is a seed which if properly nourished will grow up into the mature expression of what is within, as naturally as an acorn (which looks nothing at all like an oak tree) becomes an oak tree under the right conditions. So a child/new believer will (under the right conditions) grow up to become exactly the person his Heavenly Father created him to become. Part of our mission is to lay a personal prophetic foundation of redemption and restoration through identity/security, purpose/self-worth, and destiny/significance.

Powerful people affect the good of the community. They lay strong foundations for the 'common good', which means the flourishing and fulfilment of each person. To live an excellent adventure, we need strong foundations of honour, identity, value and worth of the individual family unit and the city (Romans 4:17). Good foundations call people out from negative self-beliefs, out from merely conforming to the culture around them, calling them into Godly true belief about who they are and why they are. Purpose is about doing and making a difference. It flows out of being created in the image of God. It is about doing creative and fulfilling employment, not the mundane or boring kind. Purpose is about adding value, making a difference. Destiny calls us into the big picture to see beyond survival and mere existence. Destiny calls us to live for things outside of ourselves and ultimately for eternity – who we are and what we do matters and makes a difference.

Powerful leaders and adventurers envision people to be world changers. People who build on strong foundations don't just live safe lives and let boredom set in through routine mundane living. The community cannot function without each member playing his/her part to the full, from doctors, nurses and staff, police, justice, teachers, students, car mechanics, parents, businesses, refuse collectors (all sorts) to post/delivery people and so on. Each and every person is essential to the smooth and effective running of any community or society. That is some of your adventure.

"The credit goes to the man actually in the arena whose face is marred by dust sweat and blood" said Theodore Roosevelt. Having strong foundations empowers us when we embark on Christian action and embrace the cross and resurrection, and thus confront the domain of Satan and all powers of evil. The deadly reality of the battle is experienced in the struggle for justice for the needs of the poor and oppressed, the sick and the ignorant. Even those who struggle for creation, its creatures and environment experience great opposition, just as much as those who struggle evangelistically to bring people to faith in Christ as saviour and Lord and plant churches. Strong foundations enable us to hold firm in the midst of opposition, challenges and difficulties. Often by the time you reach 70 people say you've had a good life, but as someone once said, "Don't talk about my life in the past, I have a future, a hope!" (Jeremiah 29:11).

Good foundations enable us to flourish as we grow older. Picasso did his best work in his nineties; Thomas Edison discovered the light bulb in his eighties. Pascal wrote: *"If God does not exist, one will lose nothing by believing in him, while if he does exist one will lose everything by not believing."*

Simon Sinek writes: *"It needs a very special and rare partnership between one who knows WHY and those who know HOW. It is not an accident that these unions of whys and hows often come from families or old friendships."*

The foundations of our adventure mean we are to be people who start with our destiny, not our circumstances. Our history is our experiences, not our foundations or our destiny. Our history is to become a stepping stone to the greatness inside us. Our past is not our future. Let us allow it to shape us into something beautiful as we live our adventure. Accept your starring role in your story. Overcome obstacles, challenges and apathy. I encourage you to seek to understand God's pre-set destiny for you. Then live life in all its fullness. Don't be like powerless people and allow your family of origin, circumstances or events so far in your life to conspire to stop you being the hero God designed you to be.

Thoughts for your consideration

What are the key foundations that you are building your relationships on? How do your leadership team/those you mentor answer this?

Do you understand the importance of building on foundations, rather than culture? What does this look like in your situation?

What are the foundations that you are leading from? Is your team/those you mentor fully on board with these foundations – why/why not? How do you know?

How often, and how, do you test the foundations in your life, marriage and ministry? What does this look like? Do you and your team/those you mentor also do this openly and honestly?

How, in your own words, do good foundations enable you to finish well?

What has spoken to you most in this chapter?

CHAPTER 13
Strengths and weaknesses

Generally people are very proud and confident of their strengths, but less assured about acknowledging their weaknesses. Vulnerability is vitally linked in God to being powerful. Vulnerability is about understanding ourselves and not being afraid to be real about ourselves around others. It is also about other people knowing and understanding you, your strengths and weaknesses.

Once we are aware of our weaknesses, we can use them to our advantage. A lady takes her pet chihuahua with her on a safari holiday. One day the chihuahua wanders too far and gets lost in the bush. It soon encounters a very hungry-looking leopard. The chihuahua realises he's in trouble, but noticing some fresh bones on the ground he settles down to chew on them with his back to the big cat. As the leopard is about to leap, the chihuahua smacks his lips and exclaims loudly "Boy, that was one delicious leopard. I wonder if there are any more around here." The leopard stops mid-stride and slinks away into the trees. "Phew" thinks the leopard, "that was close. That evil little dog nearly had me."

A monkey nearby sees everything and thinks he'll win a favour by putting the stupid leopard straight. The chihuahua sees the monkey go after the leopard. He guesses that the monkey might be up to no good. When the leopard hears the monkey's story he feels angry at being made a fool off. The leopard offers the monkey a ride back to see him exact his revenge. The little dog sees them approaching and fears the worst. Thinking quickly, the little dog turns his back. He pretends not to notice them. When the pair are within earshot, the chihuahua says aloud, "Now where's that monkey got to? I sent him off ages ago to bring me another leopard."

An effective adventurer or leader ensures their weaknesses are covered by others. In turn, their strengths cover others. It is important that we know, identify and are vulnerable with others about our weaknesses. Understand the 'shadows' that directly impact upon you your life attitude and behaviour. When we confess them in a secure environment, we allow others to cover them with and for us. Conversely, we need to know our strengths; then we can exercise them for the growth and blessing of others. Don't judge your life from your start or mid-point – live the adventure.

"Nothing fails like success" wrote the historian Arnold Toynbee. In other words, when you face a challenge and your response is equal to the challenge, that is a success. But once you have a new challenge, the old, once-successful response may no longer work. The non- adventurer calls this a failure. In the eye for an eye and tooth for a tooth scenario, life is about fairness. You treat me well and I will treat you well; but if you don't, look out! It is a form of powerless living and relates to living out of our weaknesses instead of our strengths.

I read somewhere that great bosses play chess, not draughts. Think about the difference. In draughts, all the pieces are basically the same. That's a poor model for an adventurer or for leadership, because nobody wants to feel like a faceless cog in the proverbial wheel. In chess, on the other hand, each piece has a unique role, unique abilities and unique limitations. People on an adventure, like powerful bosses, are great chess masters. They recognise what's unique about each member of their team. They know their strengths, weaknesses, likes and dislikes. They use these insights to draw the very best from each individual. People are either limited or defined by their weaknesses, instead they utilise their strengths.

Are you confined by your strengths and weaknesses? Here are five steps to consider in developing your creative process to make the best use of your strengths:

1. State the problem clearly. What is wrong? Be as precise as you can. Vague problems are more difficult to solve. Is it a problem with you your environment, others, your thinking?

2. Set a specific goal. What is it that we really want to happen?

3. Generate as many ideas as possible. The more ideas you have, the better. Force yourself to list ten options. Brainstorm. Have fun. Be outrageous. Challenge the rules. Be off the wall. Use your intuition. Ask a lot of questions. Forget "realism" for the moment. Try crazy associations: How is this problem like an elephant?

4. Narrow your list down to the one best idea.

5. Take action! Do it now. Go for it. Many of the most successful people made it with just one outstanding idea.

Some lessons I've learned from my adventure of thirty years of living an adventure in full time Christian ministry:

1. Know God personally and intimately and keep close to Him – prayer & worship
2. Remember He is God and you are not!
3. Never allow anything to be confidential – keep no secrets from your elders/wife.
4. Don't gossip – be wise who you talk to about what.
5. If you do something wrong, admit it appropriately.
6. Don't meet a person of the opposite sex on their own – if you have to, meet them in a public place and tell someone about the meeting in advance and afterwards.
7. Remember it is God's church, not yours – let Him lead.
8. Constantly GROW in character in the word in the Spirit & spiritual gifts/fruit and in life.

9. Be a servant leader – love God, love people and love the word.

10. Guard against gossip – be open, honest and real about issues in life.

11. Preach to build, not to pull down. Don't just preach your favourite issues or to correct some people – build up, don't tear down.

12. Ensure you work as a team with your leadership team – keep learning and sharing together.

13. Stand lovingly firm against manipulation/control.

14. Be true to yourself, to your values and to God's heart.

15. Handle your finances well – live by faith, avoid debt.

16. Work hard – be self-disciplined, don't waste time but do have fun.

17. Plan at least one year ahead if you can, where you can.

18. Know your goals and be flexible, but don't be sidelined by others' goals not agreed with you. Goals need to be personal – day, week, month, year, five year and church – month year, etc.

19. Own God's (your) vision in your heart, not just in your head or as a 'strapline'.

20. Mt.18: Church Discipline is church discipline, not elders' discipline.

21. Remember you were saved by grace, not works or law – spend your time wisely, make time for you (and your family).

22. Nothing is THAT urgent! Be led by the Spirit. not need – learn the difference between the "urgent" and the important. remember what the important is.

23. Ensure you work as a team – do not allow yourself to become a one-man ministry.

24. Enjoy God, church, life and people.

25. Leaders are readers. Keep allowing your leadership skills, your mind and thinking to be stretched, but don't be tossed around by the latest trend or idea.

26. Remember God has appointed you to lead, so lead. If you are leading the church spiritually before God, it is your responsibility what happens, not that of a member or visitor or visiting ministry (Hebrews13:17).

27. Don't let fear or conflict intimidate you.

28. Prophecy and Spiritual gifts are under your authority. Prophecy must be weighed and tested against God's word; character and the relevance etc.

29. Never let theology be mere theory – it is the study of God. Know Him, love Him.
30. Be accountable for your life with others, (seek accountability – make it happen as much as you can).
31. Understand the power of story to influence others.
32. Demonstrate your own limitations; be real, but also encouraging, overcoming etc.
33. Understand the reality of Spiritual warfare, the world, flesh and the devil – submit to God AND resist the devil.
34. Communication, communication, communication.
35. Know your own strengths and weaknesses and those of your leadership team, and keep open, honest and real interaction over them with your team and others not directly involved in your ministry.
36. Recognise the reality of isolation and loneliness because of your leadership position and calling, and ensure you protect yourself against it and cover it in positive ways with others.
37. Cultivate an honour culture,
38. Be open, authentic and vulnerable.

39. Own your mistakes and confess your sins one to another.

40. Confront only in a spirit of gentleness; constantly display the fruit of the Spirit.

41. Being saved by grace means you are "unpunishable" – justified by grace and faith (Rm. 8:20). This means you live without punishing, judging or criticising others and without punishing yourself.

42. You are a hero in God's Kingdom – an adopted, called and chosen son.

43. You live from Heaven to earth by the Spirit.

44. You are predestined to life – death has no part in you or over you.

45. You can never earn or deserve your salvation, but you can live in it with joy and thanksgiving.

46. Keep short accounts.

47. Address issues; be powerful and proactive.

48. Start your preach, and your week, with the end in mind.

49. Keep growing – your walk with God; yourself; your marriage; your relationships; those around you who you can influence.

50. Train others to do your 'job'.

The sea was rough, the storm was fierce and visibility was poor, and a tense radio conversation took place between an American and an Irishman.

"This is Captain Jones of SS *Montana*. Adjust your course 15 degrees north to avoid a collision!

This is Mr O'Malley – "No, you adjust your course 15 degrees south!"

Jones: "You will divert your course 15 degrees north immediately!"

O'Malley: "Negative, captain – repeat, I'm not moving anything – adjust your course – over."

Jones: "We are SS *Montana*, the second largest ship in the North American fleet – now adjust your course immediately or face the consequences!"

O'Malley: "Captain, this is a lighthouse. Your call!"

Aggressive people are ultimately living from their weaknesses. They are powerless people.

Freedom involves choices. Knowing your strengths empowers you to make good Godly choices of, for and out of love. This ensures we are not unduly influenced by others or circumstances. To live an effective adventure, the only person you should control is yourself. When you live confident in who you are, you know no one and nothing can make you behave in a way contrary to your values, beliefs or vision It is said that no one else's self-worth lives inside another. We are not to be over influenced by feelings, circumstances or events. You came into this relationship with God by an encounter with Him. God invaded your space. He is the original space invader. He brought you into an encounter with Him. Now you're learning how to live out that encounter in a truly great adventure. You are learning to think like Him, see like Him, speak like Him, act like Him and become like Him. *'Your goal in this life is to live out what it is to be made in His image"* – Graham Cooke.

To grow, don't isolate yourself because of your weaknesses. Be and live as a community of God's people. In my adventure, I am a part of a community of blood-bought people on a journey towards blessing and abundance. The kingdom is both here, local, national, global (in the church) and in the future (in heaven). Fear of exposure separates and isolates. Knowing and even being comfortable with our weaknesses is at the very heart of the doctrine of the church. Luther spoke of the 'priesthood of the believer', rejecting the need for any intermediary between the individual believer and God. Our adventure is not about being perfect, otherwise no one could embark on it. The even more radical reformers centred their understanding on their relationship with God, on community, not on the individual. They saw the Protestant model as excessively individualistic. For them it did not take into account the need for relationships between believers. We were created by a community for a community. God the Father, Son and Spirit (the Trinity) have always known fellowship with each other. We are made in the image of God for fellowship. Regrettably we don't tend to value fellowship, at least not as highly as getting our own way!

Christianity, like Judaism, is **corporate,** from its very roots. It is absolutely essential for God's children to learn to work and play together in the Kingdom. We are not to cover our weaknesses and merely reveal our strengths. The kingdom is both here, local, national, global (in the church) and in the future. Communities are formed by their stories. Everyone has a story and each story is different. However, our stories need context. We either live in the context the world gives us or the context God gives us. The world seeks to mould or conform us to an ungodly image, yet the truth is that we are made in the image of God (Genesis 1:26). Kingdom community is counter-cultural. It expresses love and vulnerability across the community unconditionally, from undeservable grace. It is willing to be open and vulnerable to others in the community, to know and be known instead of hiding and living separated lives (James 5:16). Community flows from the foundations of grace and is unpunishable (no longer in fear of being punished).

The church is on a mission (Ephesians), not just for me and my family but to change the world and the atmosphere. We are alive for the glory of God and to enjoy Him forever.

Thoughts for your consideration

Q. Think of a small group or team you are part of - your family for example. Are there dynamics present that could prevent intimacy? Inappropriate use of humour? Violation of privacy? Judgmental statements? Premature advice giving? How might you powerfully address this? What about those you mentor?

Are you able to think outside the box, ie think creatively? What does this look like? When does this happen? What about the others in your team or mentees – do they think outside the box? If not, how do they react and respond when others do?

Do you think as the world thinks, as individuals, or do you think community and Kingdom? How does this manifest in your leadership? How does this impact on your leadership team or those you mentor? How do you know?

What has spoken to you most in this chapter?

CHAPTER 14

The importance of character

You are assigned to do a job. It is regarded as the lowest of the low. What do you do? How do you live? After a while, do you decide to relive your boredom by shouting wolf (even when there is isn't one)? You figure at least it makes people come running and notice you! Alternatively, do you observe lots of stones lying around you on the ground and proactively learn how to use them as effective weapons in case your charges are attacked by a lion or bear? Do you live for the immediate? Or are you focused on your adventure?

In 1955, a forty-two year-old black woman in the southern USA, exhausted from a hard day at work, refused to give up her place in the coloured section of a transit bus to a white passenger. The driver warned her that her defiance would force him to call the police and have her arrested. But she had had enough of white bigotry. She resented being judged by the colour of her skin instead of the integrity of her heart. She steadfastly refused to move until she was arrested and charged. Her name was Rosa Parks. Rosa stepped out of the crowd and made the call. She wasn't part of a movement; there was no movement at the time. Instead Ms. Parks put her shoulder to the boulder of history, gave it a shove, and history moved. She didn't cause a movement, but she did create forward motion. Later in life, Rosa wrote: *"Without a vision the people perish, but without courage, dreams die."*

Rosa Parks is a hero in history. The day she decided to take a stand, she did it by herself against everything the culture around her was saying to be true. Perhaps we all could be a little more like Ms. Parks; courageous risk takers who persevere. To live an adventure, to be a courageous risk taker, is something I feel I need to regularly step into. Low self-esteem steals our ability to disciple nations. False humility is killing us. It strips away our boldness, our God-given anointing. If we want to be history makers, to live the adventure, I believe we need to embrace the core values of world changers. To be people of character.

Terry Virgo wrote: *"the three C's of eldership are character, character, and character"*.

CHARACTER – *"You teach what you know; you reproduce what you are."* —Leif Hetland.

Three forces shape who we are at the core of our being:
1) The input we consume;
2) The relationships we pursue;
3) The habits we acquire.

Nothing stands the test like solid character. You can handle the blast (of adversity) like a bull in a blizzard. The ice may form on your horns, but you keep standing against the wind and the howling, raging storm, because Christ is at work in your spirit. Character will always win the day. *"Fame is a vapour, popularity an accident, riches take wing and only character endures"* – Charles R. Swindoll. Character relates to identity (who you are), purpose (why you are) and destiny (where you are heading).

People who focus on finishing their adventure will say, like Stephen Covey, *"I am not a product of my circumstances. I am a product of my decisions."* To finish well it helps to have a road map – to allow God to direct you to a biblical promise or character. Then ask yourself, "What about this promise of character that speaks to me in my situation today? Why? What does the promise, or what would the Character do in my situation? Trust it to God and step out and DO IT AGAIN!" From my experience in working with or employing people the order of the following is vital. Calling, then character, chemistry, competence and finally charisma.

Calling

"For we are God's workmanship created in Christ Jesus to do good works which God prepared in advance for us to do" (Ephesians 2:10). *"The call of God only becomes clear as we obey, never as we weigh the pros and cons and try to reason it out. The call is God's idea; and only on looking back over the path of obedience do we realise what God's idea has been all along."* — Oswald Chambers.

"The secret to success is consistency of purpose" – Benjamin Disraeli.

"Moses spent 40 years thinking he was a somebody; 40 years learning he was a nobody; and 40 years discovering what God can do with a nobody." —D.L. Moody.

"Make your life a mission, not an intermission" – Anonymous.

"A ship in harbour is safe, but that is not what ships are built for." — John A. Shedd.

"The two most important days in your life are the day you are born and the day you find out why" —

Mark Twain.

"The place where God calls you to is the place where your deep gladness and the world's deep hunger meet." —Frederick Buechner.

"Twenty years from now you will be more disappointed by the things that you didn't do than by the ones you did do. So throw off the bowlines. Sail away from the safe harbour. Catch the trade winds in your sails. Explore. Dream. Discover." —H. Jackson Brown Jr.

Character

"Promises must be kept, deadlines met, commitments honoured, not for the sake of morality but because we become what we do or fail to do. Character is the sum of all that." —Howard Sparks

"The ultimate measure of a man is not where he stands in moments of comfort and convenience but where he stands at times of challenge and controversy." – Martin Luther King Jr.

"Success is final, failure is not fatal; it is the courage to continue that counts." — Winston Churchill.

"Success consists of going from failure to failure without loss of enthusiasm." — Winston Churchill.

"Humility is not about thinking less of yourself but thinking of yourself less." — C.S. Lewis.

*"The world needs men and women [...] who cannot

be bought; whose word is their bond; who put character above wealth; who possess opinions and a strong will; who are larger than their vocations; who do not hesitate to take risks; who will not lose their individuality in a crowd; who will be as honest in small affairs as in greater; who make no compromise with wrong; whose ambitions are not confined to their own selfish desires; who will not say they do it "because everybody else does it;" who are true to their friends through good and bad in adversity, as well as prosperity; who do not believe that shrewdness, cunning and hardheadedness are the best qualities for winning success; who are not ashamed or afraid to stand for the truth when it is unpopular; who can say "no" with emphasis although all the rest of the world says "yes". —Ted Engstrom, *The Making of a Christian Leader*

Chemistry
"It is not the critic who counts; not the man who points out how the strong man stumbles or where the doer of the deeds could have done them better. The credit belongs to the man who is actually in the arena, whose face is marred by dust and sweat and blood; who strives valiantly; who errs, who comes short again and again because there is no effort without error and shortcoming; but who does actually strive to do the deeds; who knows great enthusiasms the great

devotions; who spends himself in a worthy cause; who at the best knows in the end the triumph of high achievement, and who at the worst, if he fails, at least fails while daring greatly, so that his place shall never be with those cold and timid souls who neither know victory nor defeat." —Theodore Roosevelt

Competence

"Men wanted for hazardous journey. Low wages, bitter cold, long hours of complete darkness. Safe return doubtful. Honour and recognition in event of success." – Advertisement said to have been placed by Ernest Shackleton, the polar explorer.

Charisma is about influence. Whilst this can be vital, it also needs to be harnessed with the other elements.

The 10 Cs of Adventure and Leadership (Positive attributes)

Calling – they need to be "called".

Character – reliable, faithful, integrity, honesty, trustworthy;

Chemistry (Connection) – the team has to work with friends and brothers and be able to challenge and bring the best out in each other, and more importantly the church/team they serve.

Competence – being able to do the job well, with a proven track record of serving within the church fruitfully.

Charisma – elders need to have spiritual stature, be anointed by God, with a leadership gift that means people want to follow and listen.

Commitment – in it for the long haul and the hard work.

Clarity – Provide clear vision and clear trumpet sound – prophetic leading and accountability to the vision.

Church – Heart of love for the church, organisation or adventure, a servant heart and knowledge that it is God's church, not ours – live the adventure that is Christ.

Communication – open, honest, real and truthful.

Conflict resolution – Mt.18.

Children – Care for physical and spiritual ones

The 10 Fs of adventure and leadership (negative attributes)

Fear – fear that stops you acting as you should act.

Foreboding joy (Coping with past disappointments and their effect on future plans).

Futility (scarcity – is your glass half full or half empty?)

Failure (treat triumph and disaster as imposters – learning to handle failure in a Godly way).

Future – the fear of what might be can stop you living the here and now.

Finance (make it your friend – don't let it rule you and your lifestyle).

Friendship (Don't have favourites).

Freedom – seek it not just for yourself.

Focus (on solutions, not problems).

Faith – it's not the unloved that go to hell but the unsaved.

The 10 Ps of adventure and leadership (dangers)

Pride – don't over-focus on you.

Petticoats – be aware of the trap of sex.

Pennies – don't let the love of money drive you.

Power – live powerful, choosing how to act in any given situation, ensuring no one makes you do what you do not want to do). Power is not about control, intimidation or manipulation.

Powerlessness

Past (generational issues)

Passionlessness (do you have time and energy for your wife?)

Propheticlessness (You need to make time to hear God and be led by the Spirit).

Passivity (ruled by fear and shame).

Position – don't seek position above people.

Develop your character

Know that what you sow, you reap. Ploughing and planting always come before harvesting.

Ignite your purposes and passion, fulfil them with achievable steps and goals and reap rewarding results personally and professionally.

Improve work/life family/relationships balance.

Realise your potential – calling; gifting (don't be sidetracked by need – yours or others).

Better manage your money.

Accomplish more in less time.

Keep/get focused.

Strengthen relationships.

Enjoy life more in your singleness/marriage (how? plan etc).

Enlarge your vision (Prov. 29:18).

Keep/stay motivated.

Live from/out of your values and Integrate your values with work/life.

Achieve satisfying results/outcomes – leave a legacy.

People of character do not allow their identities to be stolen by the culture or other people's definitions of them. They are self-aware and can stand mentally outside themselves and evaluate their beliefs, actions and values. They can think about what they think. They can challenge their own assumptions. They are free to make their own choices. They are creative and have a conscience.

People of character seek people as "helpmates" – I see myself independent from "my side". I see you as a human being – independent from "your side".

I seek you out because you see things differently. I synergise with you. Together we create an amazing future that no one could have foreseen, using the weapon of forgiveness.

Character recognises that people often protest that they are no longer in love. However the truth is they are perfectly free to love one another if they choose.

The notion of being "in love" is passive. To love is a verb – an action.

People have the power to do loving things or hateful things to one another. They choose – they write the script. Living from character means you write your own story and you need to be willing to rewrite it if necessary – because you want it to end well.

People of character who are in conflict consider:

What's my story? Do I need to change the script?

Where might i have blind spots about myself?

How has my cultural programming influenced my thinking?

What are my real motives?

Are my assumptions accurate?

In what ways are my assumptions incomplete?

Am I contributing to an outcome – an end to the story – that I really want?

Thoughts for your consideration

Q. Think of your closest relationships at this time, one at a time. Ask yourself "is this relationship moving me closer to God or farther away? Is it helping me grow spiritually and morally or is it producing habits and attitudes that are cause for concern?" Ask your team to answer the same question and compare together openly.

What does being a leader of character mean to you? What does it look like to those around you? What about those in your team and those you mentor?

Do you live and lead according to calling, or according to the needs or pressures of the time? How is this demonstrated? What about the rest of the team/those you mentor- how do they respond? How does this manifest in your leadership meetings?

Why, in your own words, do you think that character and calling are so vital to finishing well? What about your leadership, the team? What about those you mentor?

What has spoken to you most in this chapter?

CHAPTER 15
Legacy

A man walking in the woods came across a young lumberjack working feverishly to cut down a tree. "What are you doing?" He asked. "I'm sawing down this tree," he replied. "You look exhausted, how long have you been at it?" asked the man. The young lumberjack replied "over five hours". "It looks as if your saw is a bit blunt," said the man. "It probably is after all the time I've been sawing," said the young lumberjack. "Then why don't you take a break and sharpen it?" the man suggested. "The job will be a lot faster and easier if you do." The young lumberjack replied, "I don't like sharpening, and anyway I don't have time right now, I'm too busy sawing." Leaving a legacy can make the life of those who follow more effective.

To live an adventure is to live a life beyond yourself. To live for eternity and beyond. Legacy involves encouraging, equipping and empowering those coming behind you to be even better than you are. Legacy aims to be floor, not the ceiling, for those following.

To leave a legacy requires being releasing, not controlling, and bringing freedom and responsibility to others' decisions, choices and actions. To leave a healthy legacy, never give in to the temptation to focus on today and the immediate. Always plan and prepare for what lies ahead and look out for who may follow you in leadership. Work hard for today, live for tomorrow and those who come after you. *"He is no fool who gives up what he cannot keep to gain what he cannot lose"* – Jim Elliott.

"Twenty years from now you will be more disappointed by the things that you didn't do than by the ones you did do, so throw off the bowlines, sail away from safe harbour, catch the trade winds in your sails. Explore. Dream. Discover." – Mark Twain

All of us leave a legacy. The question is – is it for good or not? How can you and I create a legacy? Steven

Covey says: "*Simply put, leadership is communicating to people their worth and potential so clearly that they come to see it in themselves.*"

To leave a legacy in God, start from what He HAS done, not from what He hasn't done. Focus and declare what God has done. Remember, He is God and you are not. Trust Him and build.

I don't know if I have ever read this statement (I can't believe it would be original to me), but I believe it to the core of my being: "Only a leader can develop another leader." (or only an adventurer can develop another adventurer)

In your adventure, you can empower others to live up to their full potential by mentoring them. A mentoring relationship empowers the mentee to grow deeper, reach higher and stretch further. It empowers because it encourages the other. It empowers because it sharpens the other. It empowers because it teaches the other – with words and actions. As William Wallace wrote, *"Every man dies. Not every man really lives."*

Michael Jordan said, "I've missed more than 9000 shots in my career. I've lost almost 300 games. Twenty-six times I've been trusted to take the game winning shot and missed. I've failed over and over and over again in my life. And that is why I succeed."

"*Strive not to be a success but rather to be of value*" – Albert Einstein.

To leave a legacy requires taking specific action – it will not just happen.

Ask your mentee to identify their ONE theme or goal for the next year, or five or ten years. Then ask them what objectives they need to accomplish that goal or adventure. Ask what they would need to continue through the year as usual, no matter what theme or goal they have.

Sometimes it helps to write down a statement to support your aim of legacy. For instance – as the Lord leads and guides me, I will continue supporting ...... and their ministry both as a brother and leader as long as I am confident that he has not compromised doctrinal truth, as long as he has not jeopardised the position of being a chosen vessel of God and as long as he remains faithful, transparent, sincere, humble and meek. Here are some warnings for aspiring leaders:

1. What you settle for becomes the culture.

2. Mediocrity isn't created. It's accepted.

3. Your actions determine their reactions.

4. Don't assume they agree just because they haven't said anything.

5. You'll never get there just thinking about it.

6. If you're the leader, they are likely waiting on you to lead or release the right to lead.

7. What the team values becomes apparent by your actions, not your words, no matter how well-spoken they might be.

Leave a legacy, mentor well, remind those who follow you that they are some of the most important and influential people alive today on Planet Earth. How do I know? How can they know this? Jesus died for them, and by His grace they are now beloved children of God on the mission of the Kingdom. They are born again to make a difference in a fallen world. They can now live powerful lives. They are able to reject living passive, aggressive or passive/aggressive lives. They have been filled with the same Holy Spirit that raised Christ Jesus from the dead. They are able to do exceedingly abundantly far beyond all they can ask or think, according to the power at work in THEM. C.J. Mahaney said: *"Never be content with your grasp of the gospel. The gospel is life-permeating, world-altering, universe-changing truth. It has more facets than any diamond. Its depths man will never exhaust."*

A vital part of leaving a legacy is understanding the significance of remembrance. Dr. Alistair Stewart-Sykes comments *"...remembrance involves the participation of the individual and makes certain that the blessings appropriated in history are made authentic for the present."* ie DO IT AGAIN! Remembrance in the Bible is much more than a mental exercise. It leads to a new appropriate action. The Disciples failed to take the miracle of feeding the 5000 into the next situation they faced. One of them should have said, "Remember what happened and let's do it in this situation". Jesus said, "Do this in remembrance of me." Not as a memorial, but as a dynamic example to live out of. Do this in remembrance, ie know you are forgiven and redeemed. Live free as a loved son; a joint heir with Christ. Remember, who you now are is not who you once were. The world, the flesh, the devil are constantly try to point you back to your past. Exercise the weapon of forgiveness!

Jesus reminds us of the past to go forward. To leave an effective legacy, remind yourself and those you mentor - NOW you are **forever forgiven,** redeemed, unpunishable; loved chosen sons. Stop worrying about failure. Start doing. Realise some risks are too important not to take.

The Bible is full of the concept of memorial and remembrance. Hebrew culture did not simply *think* truth - they *experienced* truth. The deed was more important than the creed! Why? So they would do it again! But fear caused them to be passive and retreat behind the law. To live an effective adventure, we need to stop worrying about failure and start doing. Remembrance is about action, not passivity. The Bible is written not as a mere history book but as HIS STORY. A story for you to repeat and make your adventure grow. God asks, will you trust me through your life as your forefathers did? The Bible is not just history or even just His-story; story it is to be YOUR story – do it again! Consider Daniel 3:16-19; Luke 22:42; Hebrews11:32-9 and DO IT AGAIN. It was said of John the Baptist that he was least in the Kingdom, ie he was the first and everyone else was to build on his work and ministry. Jesus said, "Greater things than these will you do" (John 14:12). Testimony means DO IT AGAIN! History is not simply a cascade of names and dates divorced from meaning and relevance. *It is the story of our world* and we are to learn from it. There's an old adage suggesting that the one who forgets history is condemned to repeat it. God of Abraham, Isaac and Jacob. (Exodus 3:6; Acts) Build one on another. Do it Again! Abraham received the promise. Isaac was the promise. Jacob learnt to live out the promise despite his failings Do it again! (Hebrews 12:1) Old Testament and New Testament heroes are cheering us on – They've run their race so that we can carry their baton to the finish line. Do it again and again! Keep being and living powerful adventurous lives. Who is your Biblical hero? –

According to Jesus, greater works than these will you do! Will you? Why not start today?

LEGACY (Matthew 7:24-7): We have one life but a choice of two ways to live it:

1) Exist and see what comes – ie build on sand or

2) Lay a legacy for others to live from, ie build on rock.

Those who follow us will walk on the altars we build; if we build material altars, that's what they are likely to worship. Being alive means we are telling a story – our lives.

What legacy do you want to leave? It could be a legacy of wise political engagement. Is it possible? Do not allow the world's culture or pressure to form you. Rather respond in a way that reflects and honours Jesus.

1. Be prophetic. Our first loyalty is to Jesus and His kingdom – not to any political party. We are to lay and build on Godly foundations values culture and beliefs.
2. Be value driven.
3. Be loving.
4. Be prayerful. Seek God's wisdom revelation and solutions not merely natural ones!
5. Be peaceful.

6. Be courageous. *"Life can only be understood backwards, but must be lived forward"* Soren Kierkegaard. *"All their life in this world ….. had only been the cover and title page; now at last they were beginning Chapter One of the great story which no one on earth has read: which goes on for ever; in which every chapter is better than the one before."* C.S. Lewis, *The Last Battle*.

Thoughts for your consideration

What are you doing to raise up a new generation to follow and take over from you? What about those in your team and even those you are currently mentor? Encourage those you mentor to think beyond themselves to their mentees.

How will you know when it is time to pass your area of leadership on to someone else? How important is it to you to leave a legacy? What from your perspective would a successful legacy look like?

What will you do to ensure that you do finish well? What about those in your team and those you are currently mentoring?

What has spoken to you most in this chapter?

CHAPTER 16

To Eternity and Beyond!

In the film *The Jungle Book*, Mowgli doesn't want to leave the jungle and go to the man village. He tries everything to avoid going. Then he meets a beautiful girl, and his heart is changed. Everything depends on the focus of our heart. A Franciscan once said: *"Once you come to know the Love of Jesus Christ, nothing else in this world will seem as beautiful or desirable."*

To live an adventure and finish well, we need to know how to live in these end times. Like Mowgli, we need love to impact our heart. Richard Foster observed that so many Christians are trying rather than training.

Living a Christ-centred life is like driving a car. When you start, you don't know what to do. But once you've been trained, it becomes natural and you can do it well without thinking. Douglas Willard says a similar principle occurs in living complete in Christ. Changes and developments in character that were deemed impossible become possible and realised through the power of Christ's Spirit in us.

Although this side of eternity there is no final graduation, each year there should be a growth in the knowledge and love of God. For many believers Christ is present in their lives, but His Lordship is resisted. For others, Christ is prominent in their lives but there are still areas where Jesus is not daily directing them. If we are to live an adventure and finish well, we need to make Christ pre-eminent as the focus of our being and pursuits, so confident in God's goodness that even when we are faced with evil and suffering we continue pursuing our adventure and finish well. We must grow in the assurance of God's love. Also to be free and able, like Joseph, to simply do what we know to be right, irrespective of what others do or have done to us, using forgiveness as a weapon.

How do we live in the end times? Spiritual discipline enables us to live differently, to conquer negative habits of thought, word, feeling and action that try to inform and govern our lives. Sister Agnes said: "if we don't deal with our monsters, we will kill people". Jesus needed solitude and silence and intimacy with his Father in order to minister in this world – so do we!

As followers of Christ, God is our master – we own nothing. We are not here on our own business. Am I the Lord of my life, or is Christ? Do I live by the great 'I will' (Isaiah 14:13-14) or in the words of Frank Sinatra "I did it my way"; or the great thy will (Matthew 6:10 Mark 14:36)? We face this decision many times every day. People are eternal beings who are appointed to a resurrection of life or a resurrection of judgement. It is vital that we see God as He is. We need to see Him through His Son (Matthew 11:27; John 14:9). The Spirit and word of God are our primary means of God's revelation of Himself.

Live to impact the world around you. Live in the power and leading of the Spirit in you. Guard your inner life, hearts, conscience, mind, emotion and will. They become troublesome and wayward if they are not submitted to the rule and authority of Jesus. Henri Nouwen says: *"When we say I have always been impatient; I guess I will have to live with it".* We are being fatalistic. Fatalism is the attitude that makes us live as passive victims. Faith on the other hand can transform us from victims of darkness into servants of light.

Be aware; hence the challenge of writing this book. It will not be easy to live your adventure and finish well. You and I exist to magnify Jesus Christ. I am on this planet for one ultimate reason: to do whatever I can to make Jesus Christ known and treasured – a knowing and a treasuring that accords with his infinite beauty and immeasurable worth. We believe and pursue the truth that God is most glorified in us when we are most satisfied in him. But we also know that in this life, joy in God is never unmixed with sorrow. Never.

Paul in Colossians 1 described the majesty of Christ:

In Him we have redemption the forgiveness
of sins (v 14).

He is the image of the invisible God.

He is the first born of all creation – that is, He is the specially-honoured first and only Son over all creation.

By Him all things were created in heaven and earth visible and invisible, whether thrones or dominions or rulers or authorities.

All things were created through Him.

All things were created by Him.

He is before all things.

In Him all things hold together.

He is the head of his body, the church.

He is the beginning.

He is the first born from the dead.

In everything; He is pre-eminent.

In Him all the fullness of God was pleased to dwell.

He reconciles all things to Himself, whether on earth or in Heaven.

He makes peace by His blood.

Paul tells us these things because *he* wants us to see and feel that our salvation in Christ is invincible. When Christ died for sin and rose again "he disarmed the rulers and authorities" (Col. 2:15). If you have put your trust in him, here is what he says about you in Colossians 3:3–4: "You have died and your life is hidden with Christ in God. When Christ who is your life appears, then you also will appear with him in glory." You are secure forever in Christ. Nothing can separate you from the love of Christ, not even the most vicious cosmic powers (Romans 8:38–39).

Constantly develop your emotional intelligence and empower those involved in any way in your adventure to develop theirs.

Manage yourself. This doesn't mean suppressing feelings, rather noticing them. Then reflect on your reactions and reframe the situation. Recognise the value of different perspectives of others. Different viewpoints allow us to see something others do not notice.

Managing conversations builds on the reflections each person has about their initial reaction and takes some moment-by-moment awareness when you're communicating. If you can learn to take a pause before making a potentially contentious remark, you are more likely to find the right words to express your views without sounding defensive or on the attack.

Managing relationships is a strategy best done before addressing hot topics. Getting to know each other as people, including other's goals and concerns, helps everyone recognise that each of us is more than our specific views. It is important to build trust grounded on real experiences with each other. Invest in relationships that are key for the success of the adventure. Ideally, team members can monitor the quality of interactions during team discussions and intervene.

Conflict will arise in teams, but we have a choice in how we respond. Emotional intelligence can help you cool conflict when it appears.

REMEMBER – Develop vision and a positive outlook for your future.

a) Ask, why me? Spend 60 seconds at the start of each day – why are you so blessed? Remind yourself who you are in Christ.

b) Who cares? The question is meant to tease out our values and mission. It is to be answered with: "I choose to care and I choose to thrive because…" eg a mission statement could be: "I choose to care and I choose to thrive because God demands it, my family deserves it and the world is starved for it."

c) At the end of your day ask, "What more can I do to ensure that tomorrow is better than today?" This allows you to form a strategy for tomorrow.

So Live your adventure – Live His adventure – The best is yet to come!

Thoughts for your consideration

How secure are you in God?

What are you doing to continually grow deeper in God and be able to resist in the evil day?

It will not be easy, but it is a great calling to live your life as an adventure and finish well – do you accept this commission?

What has spoken to you most in this chapter?

BIBLIOGRAPHY

The Bible

No Well-Worn Paths – Terry Virgo

Relational Leadership – Walter C. Wright

Emotionally Healthy Spirituality – Peter Scazzero

Changing Values – David Attwood

Mere Christianity – C. S. Lewis

The Lord of the Rings – J. R. R. Tolkien

The Seven Habits of Highly Effective People – Stephen Covey

A People Prepared – Terry Virgo

A Mind for God – James Emery White

Future Grace – John Piper

Man's Search for Meaning – Viktor E. Frankl

Surprised by Hope – Tom Wright

www.ingramcontent.com/pod-product-compliance
Lightning Source LLC
Chambersburg PA
CBHW060150050426
42446CB00013B/2759